Anima Christi

Anima Christi

Reflections on Praying with Christ

ROBERT JEFFERY

DARTON · LONGMAN + TODD

First published in 1994 by
Darton, Longman and Todd Ltd
1 Spencer Court
140–142 Wandsworth High Street
London SW18 4JJ

© 1994 Robert Jeffery

ISBN 0–232–52056–9

David L Fleming's translation of the *Anima Christi* prayer
is taken from *The Spiritual Exercises of St Ignatius: A Literal Translation
and a Contemporary Reading* by David L Fleming,
published by the Institute of Jesuit Studies, St Louis, Missouri,
and used by permission.

Scripture quotations are taken from the Revised English Bible
© Oxford University Press and Cambridge
University Press 1989.

Phototypeset by Intype, London
Printed and bound in Great Britain by
Page Bros, Norwich

In memory of
Christopher Bryant SSJE
A wise man, a good friend, and
a pastor of many

Contents

Contents

Preface

This book has evolved over a period of some six years. Various parts of it have been preached as sermons, firstly as a Good Friday Devotion in St Bartholomew's Church, Tong; then as a Three Hours Devotion in Lichfield Cathedral. The material has also been used as a course of Lent Lectures, delivered first in Kidderminster and then in Worcester Cathedral. Finally it was delivered as Pastoral Addresses for former students at Ripon College, Cuddesdon. I am very grateful to Mr Martial Rose, Bishop John Waller, the Revd Beaumont Stevenson, Fr David Campbell SSJE and Sister Lavinia Byrne, who helped me with some of the source material. I am particularly grateful to the Revd Dr Gordon Wakefield, who read the manuscript and made some very helpful suggestions.

I am very grateful also to Mrs Jan Barnes for typing the manuscript, along with all her other responsibilities.

All biblical texts are taken from the Revised English Bible.

ROBERT JEFFERY
Worcester 1993

The text of the prayer

Anima Christi sanctifica me
Corpus Christi salva me.
Sanguis Christi inebria me.
Aqua lateris Christi lava me
Passio Christi conforta me
O bone Jesu exaudi me
In tua vulnera absconde me
Ne permittas me separari a te.
Ab Hoste maligno defende me.
In hora mortis meae voca me
Et jube me venire ad te.
Ut cum sanctis tuis laudem te.
In saecula saeculorum.   AMEN

J H Newman's translation

Soul of Christ, be my sanctification,
Body of Christ, be my salvation,
Blood of Christ fill all my veins;
Water of Christ's side wash out my stains;
Passion of Christ my comfort be,
O Good Jesu listen to me,
In thy wounds I fain would hide,
Ne'er to be parted from thy side,
Guard me, should the foe assail me,
Call me when my life shall fail me,

Bid me come to thee above,
With thy saints to sing thy love
World without end.   Amen.

Modern translation by David L Fleming SJ

Jesus, may all that is you flow into me
May your body and blood be my food and drink.
May your passion and death be my strength and life
Jesus with you by my side enough has been given
May the shelter I seek be the shadow of your Cross.
Let me not run from the Love which you offer,
But hold me safe from the forces of evil.
On each of my dyings shed your light and your love.
Keep calling to me until that day comes,
When, with your saints, I may praise you for ever.

Introduction

When I was eighteen I came across a copy of John Henry
Newman's *Meditations and Devotions*. I kept it with me
during my two years' National Service, which I spent
mostly in Germany. In this book was Newman's translation
of the *Anima Christi*. I had not encountered the prayer
before. I have used it ever since and so make no apology
for using Newman's translation, which is not the most
common one.

I have subsequently discovered that the prayer has a
long and complex history. The simplicity of the language,
and the repeated phrase (like St Patrick's Breastplate)
have made it easy to use and remember. It has now been
in use, not only among those who share in Catholic devotion, for over six hundred years. Over the years the words
have remained the same but the context in which the
prayer has been used has changed greatly. Is it the same
prayer, given that the context has changed so much? I
can simply express what it means to me. First let us look
briefly at the history.

In 1880 the palace of Alcazar in Spain was being
cleaned. A large amount of whitewash was being removed
from the walls. Over one doorway was found, instead of
an Arabic text, a Latin inscription. It had been put there
in 1364 when the palace had been restored by Moorish
workmen. Not only was it a Latin inscription: it was also
a Christian one. It turned out to be (with some words
indecipherable) the *Anima Christi*. So we know that the
prayer was in use in Spain by 1364, and we can go back

even earlier. Pope John XXII granted an indulgence in 1330 to those who recited the *Anima Christi* at the elevation of the Consecrated Host in the Mass. It is thought that John XXII issued this indulgence from Avignon.

There is also a reference from the same period in the diary of a German nun called Margaret Ebner (1291–1351). She was one of a group of people who had been influenced by John Tauler of Strasbourg who established a 'holy society' called 'The Friends of God'. In her diary for Christmas 1344 Margaret Ebner described how she sought to identify with Jesus's suffering by saying the Lord's Prayer for each day of his life and inserting after every fifty *Pater Nosters* the *Anima Christi Sanctifica Me*. Similarly, that book of instruction to Christians living a solitary life, *The Ancrene Riwle*, published in the thirteenth century, has another reference. After giving instruction about the elevation of the Host in the Mass the book gives a long prayer which in the middle has the phrase, 'Wilt thou come into my heart and inebriate it', which is a clear reference to the *Anima Christi*. Also from the same period, *The Book of the Poor in Spirit*, written in Germany in 1350, speaks of being intoxicated by God.

This form of devotion, which lays emphasis on the physical wounds of Christ and which subsequently led to devotion to the Sacred Heart (in Puritan as well as Catholic writers), has been traced by G L Prestige back to the twelfth century. St Bernard of Clairvaux writes in one passage: 'They pierced His hands and His feet and cleft His side with a spear; and through these openings I may suck honey from the rock and oil from the hard stone; that is, I may taste and see how gracious is the Lord . . . the privacy of His heart is exposed through the clefts of His body.' Prestige points out that this was an entirely new form of devotion: 'The feeling for Christ as love's tortured victim is something altogether new.' It was seen to be justified, as were the Ignatian Exercises later, as drawing the disciple up to a higher plane of devotion, rather than concentrating purely on the physical.

In 1487 when King Henry VII was at Winchester, his first son was born. Prince Arthur was baptised and confirmed in one service just after his birth by the Bishop of Worcester. In order to celebrate the event the King was entertained by part of a mystery play performed by the Cathedral Choristers. It was called *Christus descensus Infernos* (Christ descends into hell). In this version, but in no other version, the Christ who descends into hell is called 'Anima Christi' in an unusual reference to the prayer. This character binds Lucifer into hell and takes back his own body for the Resurrection.

St Ignatius Loyola (1491–1556), the founder of the Jesuits, recommended the use of the *Anima Christi* at the beginning of every meditation in his *Spiritual Exercises*. This put the prayer into a very different context.

Bishop Lancelot Andrewes, that great Anglican preacher and man of prayer (1555–1626), has a version of the *Anima Christi* in his *Preces Privatae*. This version has reference to the strips of Christ to heal and the sweat of Christ to refresh, which are not normally included.

John Wesley translated a version of the *Anima Christi* from German in a hymn. The first and third verses give a clear picture:

> I thirst, thou wounded Lamb of God,
> to wash me in thy cleansing blood,
> to dwell within thy wounds; then pain
> is sweet, and life or death is gain.
>
> How blest are they who still abide
> close sheltered in thy bleeding side,
> who life and strength from thence derive,
> and by thee move, and in thee live.

John Henry Newman founded Birmingham Oratory after his conversion to Roman Catholicism. He put a large crucifix on the west wall of the church and underneath he put his translation of the *Anima Christi*. It is still there today. He first published this version in the *Birmingham*

Oratory Hymnbook in 1862. In a correspondence with an Evangelical Christian, Newman enclosed his version of the prayer and headed it 'My Creed'.

The prayer, therefore, has continued in use. There are also various versions of it as hymns (both in Roman Catholic hymnbooks and the original English Hymnal). It is reported that Pope Pius XII was reciting the prayer as he died, and the Jesuit William Johnstone refers to it as a prayer emerging out of the 'spiritual void'. Modern versions of the Ignatian Exercises contain other versions of the prayer.

In this book the analysis of the prayer is in three parts. I have here followed the divisions used by Canon H A L Pass in his book on the *Anima Christi*, which was published in 1934. The prayer divides along the lines of the classical statement of the development of the spiritual life. The first is concerned with purgation and cleansing, the second with illumination and learning more of God. The third moves to the way of union in life and in death. We have learned, however, that these divisions are never clear cut: they are always spilling over into each other. Everyone's way of prayer will be cyclic, whereby these patterns are repeated several times over. God never allows us to take anything about him for granted. It is clear that St Ignatius Loyola understood this, which is why every time someone uses the *Spiritual Exercises* the whole process was to be experienced.

In some ways the division is artificial, but I hope it will be helpful in enabling the book to be used for quiet reflection. This is not a book designed to be read right through, but to be used phrase by phrase like the *Anima Christi* itself. My concern is to try and relate the prayer to the world around us, while respecting the way it has been used in the past. There are lessons which one generation of pilgrims can share with another.

The wise man brings out of his treasure 'things new and old'. We shall be poor if we stick to the old. We shall be empty if we just rely on the new.

I   PURGATION

Soul of Christ be my sanctification

The first four lines express the way of purgation. The way into prayer and deeper communion with God has to begin with a cleansing of ourselves. Many things in our lives become obstacles or hindrances to our search for God. If we are completely full of ourselves, it is difficult to find space for God. The whole pattern of the purgative, illuminative and united way illustrates the need for us all to grow in the path of prayer and not remain static. Some have also described the purgative way as the *Via Negativa* – the way of negation and self-denial – but Charles Williams has countered with his call for the way of affirmation. We have to affirm the activity of God in his Creation and seek God in our world. This requires us to turn away from ourselves. We can seek to find the wholeness, the peace, the healing, the activity of God in what is going on around us.

There is a need for growth and development in the life of prayer. So many people seem to get stuck. Praying and living are deeply intertwined, and as we go through different phases in our life so, too, we should be passing through different stages of development in our prayers. One of the great sadnesses of contemporary Christianity is that so few people seem to realise this fact. As we grow and mature, we need to grow and mature in prayer. Personal development varies from person to person and prayer needs to be related to the various types of people which we know exist. There is no one blueprint. Father Christopher Bryant drew attention to this in a paper.

Beginning with an analysis of Jung's introvert/extrovert
types of people, he argues that we should begin our prayer
by concentrating on our strengths (e.g. the intellectual
turning to meditation, the more emotional person to
affective prayer). Then we need to develop those sides of
our nature which will become negative if they are
repressed. In this way we may grow in faith. He sees
reading and reflecting on books about the spiritual life
and a full participation in Eucharistic worship as two vital
ways of bringing about a balanced maturity of person. He
writes, 'Authentic prayer must spring out of the tensions
of our actual living', which is a good starting point.

What is appropriate to people at one time in their life
may be very inappropriate at another. I found that I was
able to give much more time to prayer and meditation as
a young man than I was as a father of four young children.
Now that they are themselves growing up, the time and
space for prayer increases accordingly. Dom John Chap-
man was very wise in his adage, 'Pray as you can and not
as you can't'. This is good advice as long as we do not use
it as an excuse to do nothing.

Knowing where you are and what you need is not always
easy. We need help to find out what is the next best step
for us – we need a friend, someone experienced in the
arts of prayerful living to point us in the right way. Such
a person has a delicate task. It is very easy to manipulate
people into our own ways of thinking. It is easy to try and
mould people to our own pattern. The wise guide or 'soul
friend' does not do that. Having shared our questions and
our searching, he or she will leave us with the decisions to
make for ourselves. We cannot allow others to make
decisions for us, as such decisions cease to be our own
and give us someone to blame if things go wrong.

The 'soul friend' is one important help on the path,
but there are other forms of help. They have emerged
out of the experience and tradition of the Church down
the ages. The way we use Scripture is vital. We must
approach the Bible with the whole of our being and not

just with part of it. St Ignatius Loyola encouraged people to use their imagination as they read a passage of Scripture. We can imagine we are present at some incident in the life of Christ; we can feel it, sense it, imagine the atmosphere, the smells, and the words spoken. Imagination on its own, however, could lead us into a world of utter fantasy, so such a use of Scripture needs to be balanced by a critical understanding of the passage. This can be best done by using biblical commentaries as a way of meditation.

The sacraments are another vital element. They give us an objective sign of the love and grace of God. They are something done rather than something said, so we can enter into God's activity not just with our minds but with our whole being.

We also need the use of prayers which connect us with Christians of other times and places. The prayers which have inspired others will give help to us as well.

We can learn from the experience of other Christians. Reading about the lives of Christians is a help in understanding what lies ahead of us in the Christian path. Many people in previous generations were inspired by reading the lives of the saints. I suspect that at the present time the experiences of the lives of contemporary Christians may be of more help to us. We can read the lives and the writings of Dietrich Bonhoeffer, of Dag Hammerskjold, of Oscar Romero, or Evelyn Underhill and we can catch a glimpse of what it means and costs to be a Christian in today's world.

Our whole mind has to be engaged in the process of discipleship. Some people are attached to forms of Christianity which provide an escape from strenuous intellectual discipline. Philosophical and critical problems are put on one side and the religious life becomes much more one of emotion on its own. Then rigorous thinking and difficult questions are sidestepped in favour of feeling comfortable with like-minded people. This cannot be right. Our Lord commanded us to love God with our

whole being: 'You must love the Lord your God with all
your heart and with all your soul and with all your mind
and with all your strength' (Mark 12:30). It is our whole
being that must respond to God and if we neglect any
part of it we become spiritually handicapped. We cannot
all be academic theologians, but we can face difficult
questions and look to the academics to help us find
answers.

The Christian faith does need to have a natural progression in prayer. We can summarise this briefly. As
children we learn simple prayers. We see God like a loving
mother or father. We need a sense of safety and security
and our prayers are simple and trusting. This is followed
by a time when our minds become more alert. We start
thinking more fully for ourselves. Many questions begin
to emerge and at this point we need to pray with our
minds. It is then that meditation becomes an important
part of prayer.

We discover that we have feelings, emotions, longings
and desires. There is a sexual element in prayer: if there
was not it would not be real and it would be unhelpful
to deny it. As we become more aware of our emotions we
need to express this in prayer as in other relationships.
Emotion has a proper place in prayer and we should not
run away from it. So our relationship with God begins to
change. We establish forms of loving prayer which are
often simple and repetitive. The writers on prayer
describe it as 'affective prayer'. Prayer begins to become
simpler again.

The process does not stop here. The more we pray,
think, reflect and share our feelings, the more we discover
that the deeper awesome mystery of God is beyond our
understanding. Words become empty and meaningless.
Just as two lovers can sit in silence, so prayer becomes a
silent 'being' in the presence of God.

This is a pattern of development which prayer needs if
we are to be mature in faith. It is never a complete
progression. The pressures of life often lead us to revert

to previous patterns. Life goes backwards and forwards, and so it is with prayer. A period of deep contemplation may well be followed by a time of meditation.

We have already seen that how we pray is related to what God has called us to do at any particular time of life. My life of prayer within a Cathedral community, where prayer has been offered as a regular daily flow for over 1,300 years, is very different to my pattern of prayer as a vicar in a remote county commuter village. The prayer of a mother with children at the breast and nappies to change will be very unlike the prayer of a retired spinster. God never calls us to do the impossible.

Prayer and life are not two different things. They are part of the response of our whole being to the whole Creation and its Creator.

The mediaeval mind saw the world as a whole much more easily than we do. Those who wrote the *Anima Christi* on the arch in Alcazar would have seen it as a natural thing to do. God ruled over all as he overarched the Creation. The whole of life was a search for Christ and his holiness.

Anima Christi sanctifica me.

These words have almost always been translated 'Soul of Christ sanctify me'. Is this the best translation for our age? We have become very suspicious of the word 'soul'. The insight of psychology and psychiatry have given us a different vocabulary and we are more likely to talk about the psyche or 'the unconscious mind' than we are to talk about the soul. Modern jargon would tend to use the word only in the context of 'soul music'.

So let us start again. Take a Latin dictionary and look up the word *anima.* You will see that the word means a current of air or wind. It is the air we breathe which gives us life. Without it there would be no life. The breath of life is what *animates* us. In this way we can distinguish the soul from the body. But *anima* can also mean 'mind'. The

mind is the seat of all thought and feeling within us. We
have a string of words here:

Soul of Christ
Breath of Christ
Spirit of Christ
Life of Christ
Mind of Christ

I suspect that the word 'mind' is in some ways the richest
of these in the modern world. It is this *Anima Christi*
which is my sanctification. It is not what I do that makes
me holy. It is what the life and mind of Christ does
within me.

The *Anima Christi* has often been prayed before a crucifix. There we see the cost of an unquenchable faith in
humanity. We see the Christ crowned with thorns. We see
the thorns of man's cruelty piercing his brain, his mind.
His mind speaks to ours. Here is a picture which can sink
deep into our life of prayer.

It is my life, my mind, my spirit, which needs to be
permeated with the life, mind and spirit of the crucified
Lord. The crucified Christ is he who has entered into the
sufferings of women and men today. He has entered into
this world and been broken, poured out so that our minds
may be in his mind. Cardinal Newman had as his motto:
Cor ad Cor Loquitur – 'Heart speaks to Heart'. We can also
affirm that Love speaks to Love; Spirit speaks to Spirit;
Mind speaks to Mind.

We realise this when we discover that Jesus has entered
into our world just as it is. There is no separation of sacred
and secular. There is no divide between the religious and
the non-religious. The Bible knows of no such division.
God the Creator is the God of all – the Redeemer cannot
be less. God either rules over the whole of life or God
does not rule at all.

Soul of Christ be my sanctification.

To be sanctified is to be made holy; that means being made whole, or complete in relation to God. 'The difference between biblical and non-biblical religion,' says Dietrich Bonhoeffer, 'is that non-biblical religion is a religion of salvation and biblical religion is a faith of redemption within history.' We can see this quite simply when we compare the identical biblical story with its non-biblical equivalent. The story of the flood appears not only in the Bible but also in the Gilgamesh epic, which was found in cuneiform tablets in Babylon. Utnapshim, the Babylon equivalent of Noah, passes through the flood and at the end is received by the gods and made one of them. He goes out of this world – not so for poor old Noah: God sends him back to rebuild and replant; he has to get the world going again. He even gets drunk in the process (Genesis 9:20ff)! The Bible is a very earthy book.

God in Christ does not offer us life out of this world but redemption within this world. He offers *Shalom.* This is a vital Hebrew word meaning peace, wholeness, harmony of relationships, peace and justice for all. We see this clearly when Jesus enters the Synagogue in Nazareth (Luke 4:16–21) and proclaims the Jubilee:

> The spirit of the Lord is upon me
> because he has anointed me.
> He has sent me to announce good news to the poor,
> to proclaim release for prisoners
> and recovery of sight for the blind
> to let the broken victims go free,
> to proclaim the year of the Lord's favour.

He is bringing in the Jubilee – the fiftieth year when restitution is made, the land is redistributed, slaves are released and all can start afresh. While the Jewish law required the year of Jubilee (Leviticus 25:8–12), there is no evidence that they ever kept it. A Messiah was needed to bring it to pass. Their sanctification was just that wholeness which only Jesus the Christ can bring.

How, then, do we let the mind of Christ enter into our minds? 'Take to heart among yourselves what you find in Christ Jesus,' says St Paul (Philippians 2:5). We are to seek the mind of Christ and Christ in the Gospels tells us how to do it: 'When you pray, go into a room by yourself and shut the door and pray to your Father who is in secret' (Matthew 6:6). Here lies the heart of our faith. This is what Dietrich Bonhoeffer called the Secret Discipline (the *Disciplina Arcana*). We need to seek the time and the space to be still; to rest in the Lord; to meditate and to pray; to love God. There is within the Church, running through all the teachers and writers of prayer, a tradition of how to do this. It is never easy. Our modern world requires a discipline which is flexible rather than rigid. Daily prayer is desirable but not always possible. If we really want to pray, we shall find the time.

Such prayer needs relaxation of both mind and body. Some people pray lying on their backs, others sitting upright. Stillness is essential and bodily posture does matter. Many are discovering in Eastern religions a considerable amount of help in this direction. In the stillness we offer God our whole life. We open ourselves to let him breathe his life into us. That life is God's life; he breathes it into us as he breathed life into Adam at the Creation. This is the same life which he breathed into the embryonic Church on the first Easter Day. 'Jesus said again, "Peace be with you! As the Father sent me, so I send you." Then he breathed on them, saying, "Receive the Holy Spirit!" ' (John 20:21–22).

St John conflates Easter and Pentecost into one event, and that is often our experience. The risen Christ is always in the midst of us; he is ever breathing life. He is sending every one of us to be his people in the world. He sends us to seek and to show his peace, his wholeness, his Jubilee to all around us. We shall learn this as we find the discipline to be still and let Jesus be in the midst of us.

Just as the *Anima Christi* lay hidden behind whitewash in Alcazar, so we all need the Secret Discipline as the basis of our Christian living.

> Life of Christ
> Mind of Christ
> Breath of Christ
> Be my sanctification.

2

Body of Christ be my salvation

Dr Nathaniel Micklem, the Congregationalist theologian, writing on this second phrase of the *Anima Christi*, emphasises that everyone must have their faith brought home personally. He points to two ways in which this is done: the sacrament of the word and the sacrament of the table. Let us look at them in turn.

1. Feeding on the word

St Ignatius Loyola in his *Spiritual Exercises* developed a method of meditation which was both simple and psychologically very profound. A passage of Scripture or a basic Christian doctrine is taken as the theme. After a period of preparation the passage is read over, and you use your imagination to put yourself into the story or scene you have been considering. You then try and work out what this means for you and turn it into prayer. This method has been strongly commended and adapted by recent writers on prayer.

Body of Christ be my salvation.

The prayer asks that we may be fed and sustained by Christ. This we do by word and sacrament. Let us look a little more closely at how we may be fed by the word of God. In 1939 three Anglican curates worked hard to develop the work of the Anglican Young Peoples Association. They were anxious to introduce meditation to young people and they found a way of reducing the Ignatian pattern to a simple procedure which was easy to follow. It goes as follows:

Prepare
Picture
Ponder
Prayer
Promise

Prepare. Preparation can determine everything that happens afterwards. It is very important to learn how to be still. Find a relaxing position – many people find sitting upright in a chair with a strong back very helpful. Deep breathing can also help with the relaxation, and it can be interpreted as a way of allowing the *anima* (the breath of life, the Spirit) to enter into us. The relaxing of every limb of the body is then a good exercise. You do this by tightening and relaxing every muscle, beginning with the toes and working upwards.

There can be other aids to concentration, for instance a prayer mat, a lighted candle, an icon, a crucifix. They can all help us to focus on what we are doing. A regular ritual helps to put us in the right frame of mind. There needs to be some opening prayer, and it is here that St Ignatius Loyola suggests the use of the *Anima Christi.* The *Veni Creator* is another prayer often suggested.

Then read through the biblical passage chosen for meditation.

Picture. Try now to put yourself into the passage you have read. Identify with one of the characters in the story, be in the crowd, listen to the words being spoken to you. Try through your imagination to catch the feel of the place, the smells, the heat, the noise, the pressure of the crowds, whatever it is.

Ponder. Think about what this means to you. How does it relate to your life now? One writer suggests that the story of the raising of Lazarus can demonstrate our need for liberation from what binds us. 'Loose him, let him go' then become powerful words (John 11:44). It is this

matching of the Bible with our own world and understanding which brings us to a point of growth in prayer.
This can be a point where emotions are released or where
new understanding dawns.

Prayer. We therefore turn to prayer, and it may be prayer
of any sort. There may be acts of penitence; there may
be outbursts of love. Sometimes words in the passage
may be turned into prayer – very often words spoken to
Jesus in the Gospel may be the basis of prayer. The
famous Jesus Prayer owes its origin to the blind man
crying out, 'Lord Jesus have mercy on me' (Mark 10:47).
This may be why and how these words appear in Scripture.
They may have been recorded in the Bible just because
they were already used in prayer and public worship.

This time of prayer may be quite prolonged and may
move into the simple pattern of affective repetitive prayer
which allows all that we have been doing to sink into our
unconscious.

Promise. Prayer is not just for our own internal life. If we
are really praying to God our Creator and Redeemer, our
prayer will relate to the whole of life. There will often be
some action to follow. There may be something to do or
say, someone to see, some task to be finished, as a result
of this time of prayer. There may be some small word or
phrase which we might like to repeat throughout the day
as an act of recollection. St Francis de Sales, who was very
prone to flowery phrases, used to call this the 'Spiritual
Nosegay' – something to sniff at or cling to during the
day.

The time of meditation will probably end with acts of
thanksgiving and intercession which arise naturally out
of the process. Such an activity will probably last around
twenty minutes or half an hour. It may not be something
to be undertaken every day, but it could be something we
can find time for two or three times a week.

The basic framework outlined here can be extended in
many ways. It could be that the Scripture passage will be
read over with the biblical commentaries a day or two

before the meditation: thus the critical implications of the passage can also be borne in mind. It is very easy for people to use Bible passages to move into a world of fantasy and unreality and the use of commentaries is a good corrective to this. The linking in of prayer to our daily lives is another way of earthing our prayer.

We do ourselves a great disservice, however, if we treat Scripture too literally. We need to aim to get back to what the writers were really trying to say. We need the benefits of understanding the cultural and social background against which the biblical writers set their thoughts and words. Their world was in some ways different to our world, but in other ways it was very close to it. Human nature is not that different. The more we can understand, the more the Bible will say to us.

The Ignatian technique need not only be used by individuals. In recent years we have seen very interesting ways of using the Bible in corporate Bible study. After a careful analysis of the text, Scripture can be used as a form of role play. This enables people or groups of people to act out a biblical passage and gain new insights, not only from the role play, but also from the interaction they have on each other. A careful critical analysis of a biblical passage can provide a deeper framework for personal or corporate understanding of Scripture.

The process can be taken further still: as a result of such corporate activity a group of people then turn their understanding into an act of worship involving possibly music, movement, mime, dance and art. Thus corporate study becomes a great act of worship involving our whole being and our relationships. Corporate activity is very important. If we just pray on our own we may well forget what we have done. We are more likely to remember a part we have played, or an encounter we have entered into with others. We are fed together.

This should not surprise us. The *Corpus Christi* is the Body of Christ – the Church. The faith we share is not our own. It is the faith of the Church handed down through the ages. If we are to avoid fantasy and unreality, we need objective standards and this is achieved both by sharing our faith with other Christians and by respecting the traditions which Christians of past ages have handed down to us. We need to listen to each other so that we may be corrected and challenged. In the process we may be changing that tradition, but that is how we remain a living Church. 'We need the Church,' says Nathaniel Micklem, 'for the enlargement, the correction, the deepening of our spiritual life.'

2. Feeding on the sacrament

Corpus Christi salva me.

It is through the bread and wine of the Eucharist that we are fed with the life of Christ. The Holy Communion is a form of corporate meditation. It is an entering into the life of Christ. We are called to the Upper Room, we share with the disciples. We re-enact what Jesus did and so we enter into his life and his life enters into us.

The manner of celebrating the Eucharist is therefore very important. The whole process of Liturgical Reform during this century has had both an emphasis on the corporate nature of the Eucharist and on relating Liturgy to contemporary society and social issues. Like every human activity, Liturgy is caught up into the culture of the age. The elaborate baroque Masses of post-Tridentine Europe reflected much more the court life of, say, seventeenth-century France (being in the presence of the King) than they did the life of ordinary people. There is a very delicate balance. A large Eucharist in a Cathedral with hundreds of people is a very different thing from a quiet Communion celebration at the kitchen table in a miner's cottage. The Jewish faith has been sustained through considerable persecution because the celebrations of major Jewish festivals take place in the home. The synagogue was much more the place for teaching and preaching.

This fact may be drawing our attention to something which the Christian Church has lost, not least because of its excessive clericalisation down the ages. We need to take seriously the contention of Roland Allen that the proper celebrant of the Eucharist is the father in his own home. (Though even by now this might be seen as a sexist thing to say!) Certainly the Upper Room was an ordinary room rather than an ecclesiastical building and Scripture teaches us that Jesus was known in the breaking of bread and that the breaking of bread took place from house to house (Acts 2:46).

The Bible can help us to put the Eucharist in its proper perspective. Here St John's Gospel is very instructive. St John is the only Gospel writer who does not give us an account of the institution of the Last Supper. John states that Jesus is the Lamb of God slain at the time when the lambs were being slaughtered for the Passover meal. Yet even if there is no direct reference to the Last Supper, take a careful look at the sixth chapter of St John's Gospel. In the context of the feeding of the five thousand, St John launches into a discourse on the meaning of the Eucharist. The feeding itself takes a Eucharistic pattern. Jesus takes the food which is offered, he gives thanks, he breaks it and shares it with the people so that all are fed. This fourfold action of taking, blessing, breaking and giving is accepted by most scholars as the basic Eucharistic action. Jesus then proclaims that he is the 'Bread of Life' and draws a comparison with the feeding of the Jews by manna in the wilderness:

> I am the living bread that has come down from heaven. If any one eats this bread, he will live for ever. The bread which I shall give is my own flesh given for the life of the world. (John 6:51)

> Unless you eat the flesh of the Son of Man and drink his blood you can have no life in you. (John 6:53)

Here is a meditation on what Jesus is doing in the

Eucharist. He is giving his life for the redemption of the world. He is calling his followers to give themselves to him for the life of the world. The whole Eucharistic action is very powerful. We offer what we have and what we are. Jesus takes it and blesses it, breaks it and gives it back for us to share. Because our life and all that we are is God's life, we share together in Christ's life and receive his life in us. It is not for nothing that *Corpus Christi* refers both to the Eucharist and to the Church. We are called to become what we are. We are fed by Christ so that we can become like Christ.

So often the words, 'Do this in remembrance of me' are interpreted by the Church as meaning, 'Hold a service of Holy Communion'. I am sure that this is not what was meant. It was a call to his followers to be like him, to be people who are broken, poured out, given so that others may have life. The Eucharist is an action whereby we remind ourselves of who we are and what we are here for. Like Jesus we are to be given for the life of the world. It is the world which God loves and sustains. It is the world for which Jesus gives his life, and our sharing in the Eucharist calls us to embrace not just our fellow Christians but the whole of humanity.

The very materials of bread and wine reflect the nature of industry throughout the world. Even the materials of the Eucharist may reflect the use of slave labour and exploitation in different parts of the world. If we share the Eucharist we are called to seek for justice for all God's people. Participation in the Eucharist is therefore a profoundly political act. It is political in that it calls us to work for a just world and that it also calls us to love our enemies.

Robert Van de Weyer, now running the Little Gidding Community, gives a description in his first book, *Guru Jesus*, of how he made his first communion in a Christian Ashram in India:

I was a little nervous when I received the bread, and I

think I half expected some feeling to come over me as I swallowed it. But it was only afterwards during the period of silence that I realised the full implication of what I had done: that in a single act I have proclaimed my oneness not only with Jesus Christ himself but with all his other followers in the world, be they humble weavers in India or pinstriped members of the British Conservative Party. As a disciple of Jesus I am now bound in love to people I loathe.

He had understood what many regular churchgoers have never understood. The Eucharist sends us out in love to people we hate, despise and loathe. The Eucharist is an act of deep revolutionary significance in our divided and oppressed world. Because of this perception, Christians in many places like South Africa, Latin America and Uganda have been struggling to find ways of justice and freedom for the people they serve. The situation in South Africa has thankfully been changing. One document which contributed to the changes has been the report known as the 'Kairos Document'. Written and signed by 152 theologians of all Christian traditions, it calls for radical action by the churches to remove injustice. The document questions the validity of any theology which is not committed to the liberation of those who are oppressed. It is an essential part of the commitment to the *Shalom* (Peace) which Jesus came to bring.

To love our enemies is essential to our Christian vocation. The Kairos theologians point out that the best way to love the oppressors is, first of all, to remove the oppression. The tyrants need to be taken from power, just government needs to be established. The food Jesus gives us is as demanding and radical as that.

Feeding on the word and sacrament takes us into realms of faith which are very risky, but which bring life to others.

3

Blood of Christ fill all my veins

Devotion to the precious blood of Jesus was something which developed in mediaeval times. It is reported that in 1247 King Henry III received a vase of Christ's blood from representatives of the crusading orders. Not everyone thought it was genuine. Some doubters posed the question: 'How can any of the Lord's blood exist on earth when the Saviour was bodily resurrected on the third day?' Such questions did not stop the practice. Pilgrims poured to Hailes Abbey in Gloucestershire to venerate the Precious Blood given to them by King Henry III and there have been several accounts of the sacred blood which liquified on certain feasts in the year. We can imagine the mediaeval pilgrim at Hailes incorporating these words into his devotion: *Sanguis Christi inebria me.*

Blood is a powerful symbol. Blood is life. The paschal lambs slaughtered at the Passover had their blood put on the lintel of the door so that the angel of death would pass over those houses. So, too, the blood of Jesus is poured out on the lintel of the Cross for the salvation of humanity. Blood is something we all have in common: whatever the colour of our skin, our social class, our religion, we all have red blood. Without it we cannot live. Blood-related diseases like leukaemia and the HIV virus have deep emotional concerns for all of us. Blood is a powerful symbol – if it was not, our cinema and television screens would not be so smattered with the blood of violence and horror. Our screens also show us the blood of human violence in war, terrorism and hatred. The sight of blood never ceases to shock, but too much enables us to take it for granted. When we look into the chalice of Christ's blood given for us, we might well shrink away in horror, for we see not only the power of redemption but also the capacity for hatred and violence which lies within each one of us.

That common sharing of blood is expressed in the common sharing of the one chalice in the Eucharist. Recent fears about the transmission of HIV have led bishops and others to issue rules and guidelines about how the chalice is to be handled and cleaned. All this draws our attention to the fact that sharing in the Eucharist is a risky business. It also has associations with the world around us: among the poor the cup is shared because there are not enough cups to go round; among the very rich at functions like City Livery dinners the loving cup is shared. The chalice is indeed a loving cup: we share in Christ's love for us and for each other. There is also a vulgar element which some people shy away from, but it should be common and vulgar, for we share the life, the blood, the saliva together. It is part of what it means to be human. We need to value our common fellowship with all our sisters and brothers for whom Christ died.

The use of the chalice, the common cup, is a vital part of our Eucharistic symbolism. The use of small individual cups and glasses denies much of the point of the sacrament and asserts an unhealthy individualism into what is meant to be a deep affirmation of community and communion. Hopefully those churches which introduced individual cups in the nineteenth century will gradually abandon them.

The symbolism of the juice of the grape is also important. There have been many arguments used to try and indigenise the Eucharist by using the common food and drink of the local people. During the Second Vatican Council there was a debate about the use of *sake* (made from rice) as the proper drink for the Eucharist in Japan. While 'in extremis' anything would do, the symbolism of

the red juice of the grape – pressed out as wine – is a
very powerful one. We are reminded of the blood we all
share whatever our culture or background. We stop using
the juice of the grape at the price of losing powerful
symbolism which unites us. Is the use of a more golden
wine in some Chuches a refusal to face this symbolism,
or merely a pointing to the ambrosia of heaven?

The symbolism of blood expresses an understanding of
sacrifice. The offering of blood is always to seek life for
others. The practice of blood transfusion in our society
is an example of how one person can directly help
another by the giving of blood. The whole idea of selling
one's blood, as happens in some countries, seems to be
abhorrent. The life, which is the blood, is something we
have in common. The blood does not belong to us: it is
God's gift to us and we ought to be willing to share it to
give life to others.

The film *Jesus of Montreal,* which attempts, only partially
successfully, to relate the message of the Gospel to the
modern world, tries to make this point. The film shows a
group of actors rewriting and performing a traditional
passion play on Mont Royale. In the process the spirit of
Christ seems to enter the actor who portrays him. He
begins to denounce the corruption of much modern life
and ends up being attacked, badly injured and dying. He
is rushed from hospital to hospital until someone will
care for him. He dies in a Jewish hospital and there then
follows a scene where some of his organs are transplanted
to give life to other people. This symbolic renewing of
the organs while the figure lies cruciform on the operat-
ing table is not totally convincing. It reduces the power
of the redemption wrought by Jesus to the merely physical
and thereby poses more questions than it answers. At
the same time the message of someone who dies in the
defence of justice and who gives up his life is a proper
one.

The picture is much better brought to life in the stories
of Christian martyrs. Most martyrs – unlike St Ignatius of

Antioch – are reluctant martyrs. It is their love for God spilling over into their love for humanity which leads them to denounce injustice and oppression, and so they go to martyrdom. Archbishop Romero is a very powerful example. A mild, scholarly priest, elected Archbishop of El Salvador because it was thought that he would be a soft touch for the oppressive regime, he began to see the injustice around him and saw not only that he had to serve his people but also that the way would inevitably lead to martyrdom. His sermons and his writing reveal the power of his devotion. He was martyred offering the chalice at the elevation in the Mass. The blood of Christ mingled with his own as he was machine-gunned down by a government agent.

Jon Sobrino has analysed in a very moving way the life of Oscar Romero. The more he associated with the poor, the deeper became his perception of their need and the injustices which befell them. In his book *Spirituality of Liberation* Sobrino takes this analysis further by looking at the particular characteristics of the modern martyr. He lists the thirty-six full-time Catholic workers who have been martyred in El Salvador since 1971. He points out that Christians have understood the inevitability of persecution since New Testament times. That persecution is not provoked by the followers of Christ but by the conflict which Christ himself provokes. Where the kingdom of God is proclaimed there will follow persecution: when the Church stands with the poor the powerful are threatened.

Martyrdom expresses the deep truth of the Gospel that we have to give up our life for Christ's sake. Martyrdom is implicit in the Beatitudes. Sobrino, through analysis of the words of Romero, expresses the main virtues of martyrs as being fortitude, impoverishment, creativity, solidarity and joy. Fortitude is an obvious virtue. It is expressed in the determination not to abandon the poor in their sufferings. Impoverishment implies the willingness to leave all to be with the suffering. Creativity is the way of turning oppression into opportunity. Romero stated that, if the radio was taken away from the Church, then he knew that every Christian would be the voice of the Gospel. Oppression cannot succeed. Solidarity is based on the conviction that no Christian goes to God alone. They are always part of a greater company. Joy is primarily the joy of knowing that we are doing Christ's will and going Christ's way. This spills over into our worship and our living.

Oscar Romero understood what he was doing. He saw that martyrdom itself was a form of liberation: 'If they kill me I shall rise again in the Salvadorian people. I am not boasting, I say it with the greatest humility.'

In the debate about the possibility of human free will it is the acts of the martyrs which reveal that we do possess free will, at least in a limited way. We can choose what to be, to give up our life for others or not. It is a choice only an individual can make. Romero, just days before he was killed, put it like this:

> If they carry out their threats, I shall be offering my blood for the redemption and resurrection of El Salvador ... May my blood be the seed of liberty and a sign of the hope that will soon become a reality ... May my death, if it is accepted by God, be for the liberation of my people, and a witness of hope in what is to come.

Sanguis Christi inebria me.

Newman translates this as 'Fill all my veins'. This is an expression of his desire to let the life of Christ permeate his whole being. The Latin contains a stronger image. The word 'inebriate' has the implication of drunkenness, of ecstasy and enthusiasm. There are hints here both of celebration and of excess. The best wine – the wine of Christ – has been kept until last (John 2:10). It is full, overflowing and intoxicating. It fills us with the Spirit of God.

The whole question of enthusiasm in religion is a very complex one. Some people find their spiritual experiences very overwhelming and difficult to control. From time to time in the history of the Church enthusiasm has taken over, faith becomes irrational, emotional and full of certainty. This phenomenon is seen as providing ample evidence of the power of the Spirit in the life of faith. Such enthusiasm often comes as a reaction to a dull, formal faith lacking in internal conviction, but the reaction can go too far. The need to grow and change and develop within the Christian faith is often stultified when people find something which they find emotionally satisfying and simply stick within it.

Baron von Hügel said there were three main stages of human development: infancy, adolescence and adulthood. He also argues that religion must contain the three elements of the institutional, the critical and the mystical – that these three have to be held in balance. If they are not, the institutional element in the Church may encourage people to stay in an infantile stage; or a church which emphasises the critical and the instructional but neglects the mystical will be intellectually alive but spiritually barren. Moreover, those firm in their institutional model will desperately strive to preserve orthodoxy and condemn those who are critical. As Gerard Hughes writes in *God of Surprises*: 'Undue emphasis on the institutional element . . . is likely to produce a Church of dwindling numbers, loyal, docile, uninspired, and passive members, God's frozen people.' Baron von Hügel's analysis is much more complex than this, but he is very firm that we must not undervalue the intellectual element in faith. The Church today is clearly lacking in both the critical and mystical elements. Their affirmation is vital to the future of a living faith.

The whole phenomenon which goes under the title of 'the Charismatic Movement' needs to be carefully assessed. The growth of African Independent Churches was most clearly a reaction against a faith which was culturally alien and lacking in significance for many Africans. This is partly true of the growth of the charismatic movement in the West, where faith had become over-intellectual and lacking in emotion. It was not meeting the deep needs and yearnings of many people. At the same time there has often been an overreaction, leading to the reassertion of authoritarian patterns of leadership, an overemphasis on signs and wonders as a proof of God's power, and a denial of rational faith by a reversion to a naïve, literalistic interpretation of Scripture. This has been very destructive. In our very secular culture such a reaction leads to a faith which thrives in a ghetto but does not in any way relate to society. The development of irrational faith of any sort also tends to lead to a further alienation of secular man. It makes evangelism much more difficult, if not impossible.

Some people have found a more real faith through the charismatic movement. This has led them into deeper paths of exploration. They have begun that journey of spiritual growth which we have already described. They have begun to catch glimpses of the glory of God and begun to learn of the mystery of faith. This is the invitation of the Spirit. It catches us up into the Cloud of Unknowing where the mystery of being and of God become fused. Such a vision, like that of the Transfiguration itself, sends us out to serve God's world.

There can be a wrong form of inebriation which we shall discover from its fruits. Faith is not immune from self-centredness and self-indulgence. Anyone who has witnessed the destructive effect of alcoholism, not only on the individual concerned, but also on those around them, will be aware of the problems. There can be a form of spiritual alcoholism. People become so wrapped up in their own personal spiritual experiences that they ignore others. They can become selfish and self-indulgent. Relationships can be destroyed as a result. In the end such people become far more concerned with themselves and not with Jesus Christ. It begins in that attitude which says: 'Jesus saves *me* – I know that I am saved.' It uses religion to boost the ego. It conserves rather than serves.

It seeks to get rather than give. The sacraments become a personal stimulant. Holy Communion is looked on as a sort of spiritual petrol station where you go to get topped up for the week. This is blasphemy: it is using God for our own ends. This attitude also permeates the life of many clergy, as they seek to be a success, to have large congregations, to be popular rather than simply trying to be faithful to the crucified Christ.

The true life and wine of Christ can never intoxicate us in this way. For his way is to give life for others; to die for others; to seek to serve and risk all that others may live. A faith which lacks this outgoing, loving aspect is not of Christ, for he calls us to take up our Cross and follow him.

So often this charismatic, evangelical faith expressed in many countries around the world today is also aligned with right-wing, anti-Communist policies which promote new Western imperialism. In a document entitled 'The Road to Damascus' published in 1989 a group of theologians from Latin America, Korea, the Philippines and South Africa has called on such Christians to repent and realise the implications of what they are doing. Those who are seeking to preserve the power of the imperialist West are now putting vast resources into a debased Christianity which will try and undermine liberation theology and sustain Western and white dominance. This is no dream but a harsh reality. The document analyses what is happening in terms of its idolatry, heresy, apostasy, hypocrisy and blasphemy. One characteristic of such faith is its authoritarian and fundamentalist approach to the Bible which is described as a form of slavery. Another aspect in its development is a false dualism. This is well summed up in one paragraph from the document:

It is not without reason that right wing Christians believe in antagonistic dualisms. It prevents the spiritual from influencing their material lives, it keeps God out of their political and economic interests. They say they are only interested in the soul, but in fact they are very concerned about the political and economic status quo. They want to preserve it at all costs because it benefits them. They say we must keep religion out of politics but invoke a kind of religion that supports the status quo. They reduce salvation to the soul only.

In a paradoxical way the collapse of Communism might be used as proof of the effectiveness of such an approach. At the same time it removes the need for such an approach. Here is another form of a false religious intoxication.

The new wine of Christ gives life to all. It is poured out for all and given to all. It is the voices of oppressed Christians in the Third World who can call us back to the true faith, for they know what it is to tread the wine press alone. They, like Christ, have drunk deep of the cup of suffering and he says to us as he said to the first disciples: 'Can you drink of the cup that I am to drink?' (Matthew 20:22).

Are we really in a position to say: 'We can'?

4

Water of Christ's side wash out my stains

The words of this fourth line of the prayer and the two previous lines have a strong sacramental connotation. They relate not only to the Eucharist but also to Baptism – they speak of the body, the blood and the water. Sacraments are part of the way of purgation. Baptism and Eucharist are both forms of identification with the death and Resurrection of Jesus. Baptism is a dying and rising with Christ through the water (itself a symbol both of life and death). The Eucharist is a sharing of the death and the life-giving new life in Christ. Some have argued that in the Church we have overemphasised the Eucharist at the expense of Baptism: Baptism is the prime sacrament of the Christian life, but the Eucharist has come to the centre while Baptism has remained a little on the periphery. Although it is a simple act, Baptism is a call to live a Baptismal life. It is a life of dying to self and living to God. By Baptism and Eucharist we are assimilated into the life of Christ; we are cleansed of our self-centredness by his total self-giving. There are two very interesting texts in the Johannine writings which relate to this.

After describing the death of Jesus (John 19:28ff.) he writes, 'One of the Soldiers thrust a lance into his side and at once there was a flow of blood and water' (19:34). The writer seems to be saying two things here. First of all, he is drawing a comparison between the works of Christ and the rock struck by Moses in the wilderness from which came forth life-giving water to sustain the Jews in the wilderness. Secondly, he is affirming that Jesus really died. Life had gone out of him and water and blood poured out from his side.

The first epistle of St John has a matching passage (1 John 5:6–8), which is almost a meditation on the first one:

> This is he whose coming was with water and blood; Jesus Christ. He came not by water alone, but both by the water and by the blood; and to this the Spirit bears witness because the Spirit is Truth. In fact there are three witnesses, the Spirit [*anima*] the water and the blood and these three are in agreement.

The Biblical commentators tell us that the point of these passages is to affirm that Jesus really died. This was necessary to refute the heresy of Docetism. The Docetists refused to believe that Jesus had really died on the Cross. He only appeared to have done. The Eucharist is also an affirmation of the death of Christ. Ignatius of Antioch writes of the Docetists:

> They have no faith in the blood of Christ . . . they even absent themselves from the Eucharist and the public prayers because they will not admit that the Eucharist is the selfsame body of our Saviour which suffered for our sins.

Docetism is still a dangerous heresy which thrives in our midst as we saw at the end of the last chapter. Docetism says, 'Only spiritual things matter'. It says we can ignore the hard practicalities of everyday life. All that really matters is that we should seek to be uplifted into the spiritual realm. Docetism asserts the priority of the spirit over the flesh and the blood.

It is always tempting to hide away in false spirituality. Both Third World documents, the 'Kairos Document' and 'The Road to Damascus', assert that such attitudes lead to racism, social injustice and the oppression of the poor. It is the sacraments which are a great antidote to such thinking. As St Ignatius has shown, it is the sacraments which can counter Docetism. The life of Christ, the Spirit, the water and the blood are harsh realities. In Jesus we are called to face and not ignore them. The sacraments help us to do so. Unsacramental faith allows us to ignore the world in which we are placed. The sacraments are an aspect of our belief in the Incarnation: God enters into the everyday parts of our life. We have already seen how the Eucharist has social and political implications. Baptism has as well. This is made very clear in the World Council of Churches' document 'Baptism, Eucharist and Ministry', where they point out that Christians have a common responsibility to witness to the Gospel in the whole of life. This implies not only personal sanctification and morality but also a responsibility to ensure that God's will is done in every aspect of our lives.

The sacraments are a means of personal and corporate motivation. We share together in something *done* rather than something *said*. The sacraments require us not simply to be passive recipients, but to act by using material objects. All this gives us a motivation to seek to do God's will and to be God's people. This is not an escape from life but a pressure back into life. Fr Benson of Cowley was once asked whether he sought peace through his faith. 'No,' he replied, 'only war.' In the struggle between good and evil the sacraments are the food of warfare. They remind us always of the passion of our Lord. He marks us with the Cross in our Baptism and reminds us of his wounds in the Eucharist. We come to learn that the nearer we are to Christ, the more there is to suffer. We see that more of our own nature has to be crucified: self-giving love is called out from us.

This is the way of purgation. We are to be marked more and more with the mark of the Cross through the blood and water of Christ's body. Nor is this just a personal matter: it applies to the whole Church as well. This purging is needed by the institutional Church. We need to live in a constant state of renewal and reformation. A Church which is not being continually renewed in the

life of Christ has lost its way, and we are only built up in
faith within the whole Body of Christ. The sacraments are
not personal and private – they belong to the Church.
Moreover, the whole Church is not just the Church in
this land but the Church across the world and the Church
across all time. If it is true that the nearer we are to
Christ, the more likely we are to suffer, then we live in a
very Christian age. As we look across the world we see
people suffering and dying for their faith in many lands
and cultures. The list of twentieth-century martyrs is a
very long one. There are other Christians who suffer in
more subtle ways than just the physical. There are ways
of psychological and emotional torment which are not
often perceived. The Gospel still offends. Where the prin-
cipalities and powers of this world are threatened by a
message of selfless love, they hit back, and the Church
and the individual Christian suffer.

While we see many signs of faith, we also see signs of
unfaithfulness. The Church needs to be purged of all that
is un-Christlike. It is too easy for the Church to be caught
up in the values of the culture in which it is set – indeed
it is impossible for this not to happen – but all these
values need to be judged in the light of the Gospel.
Often the Church fails to do that. In a very individualistic
culture, where society affirms the value of personal
achievement and success, it is very easy for the corporate
to be denied. This can affect the whole of our society.
The 'Kairos Document' pinpoints this issue. The Church
has failed to respond strongly enough to the iniquities of
apartheid because it has developed a false, individualistic,
Docetic spirituality. The document states that our faith
has become too individualistic and private: public concerns have been conceived to be outside Christian
concern, and this leads to a fatalistic waiting upon God.

It is precisely this kind of spirituality which, when faced
with clear moral and social evil, leaves many Christians
and Church leaders in a state of near paralysis. Divisions
of this sort have no basis in biblical understanding. The

Bible does not separate the individual from the social, or one's private life from a public life. God redeems the whole person as part of his whole Creation (Romans 8:18–24). A biblical spirituality will penetrate into every aspect of human existence and will exclude nothing from God's redemptive will.

We need a worldly holiness which, because it unites us to God, also unites us to our fellow human beings throughout the world. So we see the need for another form of purgation, which the Church has provided in one form or another. This is the practice of confession and absolution to a fellow Christian. The history of the practice of penance is a long and complex one. What began as a form of public confession by notorious sinners, who were then disciplined, became a more private discipline imposed upon most Christians. It was open to manipulation by clergy and by forms of clerical domination which were negative and unhelpful. It also led some into terrible scrupulosity. St Ignatius Loyola's first confession lasted three days and he still did not think it was adequate. Martin Luther could find in his confesison no respite for his sense of sin and guilt. It became the practice to require confession before making Communion but when Communion by the people was commended as a frequent act it became an impossible burden for both priest and people. The churches of the Reformation never totally abandoned the use of confession and the Second Vatican Council has made the procedure more informal and more mutual through the new services of reconciliation. Understandings developed through analysis and psychotherapy have added to changes in practice.

There are times in our lives when we not only need to feel cleansed, forgiven and pardoned, but also when we become aware that we have offended in some way against the whole community. This makes confession desirable. In our very individualistic age we fail to realise that what we do and say in private, what we think in our minds, may be having an effect on others. We are tightly intertwined with others, even when we do not realise it. Confession to a representative of the community makes us realise what it means to live together within the Body of Christ.

When Dietrich Bonhoeffer established his illegal Theological College at Finkenwalde to train pastors for the Confessing Church in Germany, he built in many of his insights from his experiences when visiting Anglican religious communities. In his book *Life Together*, where he reflects on the life of his community, he is very clear about the practice of confession. Confession, he perceives, breaks the circle of self-deception. It is only by open acknowledgement of our sin that we break out of ourselves and into the community. The brother to whom we confess represents the community to us and brings the forgiveness and acceptance of the community to us. Sin normally prefers to remain hidden: bringing it into the light removes much of its power. When we are willing to humiliate ourselves before another, we do so before God as well and so experience the power of Christ's forgiveness. The act of confession is therefore another way to experience the Cross. He writes:

> We cannot find the Cross of Jesus if we shrink from going to the place where it is to be found, namely the public death of a sinner. And we refuse to bear the Cross when we are ashamed to take upon ourselves the shameful death of a sinner in confession. In confession we break through to the true fellowship of the Cross in Jesus Christ.

From time to time, varying from person to person, we need to face the challenge of confession and acknowledge that our failures and sins are not only ours but that they offend against the community. We need the assurance of sins forgiven. Again we share in something done not merely said, and we break out of our enclosed world into the fellowship of the forgiven.

What of the sins of the community, however? What of

the purgation of the Church itself from its failure to be true to its Lord, from its acts of division, persecution, pride and power? All this also needs to be acknowledged if the Church itself is to break out of its own circle of self-deception. Sometimes this means that the Church must accept ridicule from the world, politicians, and the gutter press. The Church would do well to accept this in silence, for some of the ridicule is justified. When it is not justified the Church and often its clergy become the scapegoats for the anger of a sick society. Then, too, it needs to keep silence. The Church is called to go out, like the scapegoat into the wilderness, bearing the evil of others; for that is one of the healing functions of the Church. Sometimes the Church would do well to admit its failures and to acknowledge that it has made wrong judgements or acted in wrong ways. This could set a good example to others. Politicians would be much more credible if they admitted that they had made mistakes, but they are masters in blaming others for their own faults. Perhaps the Church would become more credible if it (as the 'Kairos Document' does) confessed to its false theology, its failures, its lack of perception, its weakness. Things named and in the open can be dealt with – things hidden away fester and eventually destroy the body.

If we are to be purged, our cleansing in the water and blood of Christ has to acknowledge our deeply corporate nature.

II ILLUMINATION

5

Passion of Christ my comfort be

Prayer before a crucifix is in some ways like looking into
a mirror. The more we look at the crucifix, the more we
discover about the meaning of ourselves and the love of
God for us. We learn the value which God has put on us.
We see the value he gives to all life. Such a reflection on
the suffering of Christ strengthens our faith.

Passion of Christ my comfort be.

The use of the word 'comfort' literally means to give
strength. Too often in modern usage the word means to
put at ease, to care for, thus implying that our faith is
'comfortable'. The meaning here is really the reverse.
The implication is to give us strength to follow the 'Royal
Road of the Cross' with our Lord: there is no implication
of ease or self-satisfaction. In St John's Gospel the Holy
Spirit is called the Comforter: the one who inspires us to
follow in Christ's steps. It is also the Christ of St John's
Gospel who offers his disciples the promise: 'In the world
you will have suffering. But take heart! I have conquered
the world' (John 16:33).

There is no promise of success, happiness or fulfilment
in the following of Jesus – just suffering and tribulation,
but tribulation tinged with hope and joy because Jesus
has conquered the world. Some modern evangelists and
Christian communicators use acceptance of Christ as a
means to build up present happiness, worldly success and
better relationships. That is not what the Christ of the

Gospels seems to be offering. He does offer healing and wholeness, but not by avoiding the Cross. A world full of pain and suffering looks to Jesus. The deep mystery of pain and evil is seen by many as an obstacle to faith. It is a deep mystery, but looking at the Crucified we find some clues.

When people suffer the cry goes out, 'Why should this happen to me?' Sometimes the wounds are self-inflicted. We know that smoking can cause cancer and that wrong diets can cause heart disease. Sometimes it is the community which causes disease. Bad housing or bad sewerage can lead to many illnesses. Human violence leads to war and to the victims of war. We are on the verge of learning a great deal more about the psychosomatic nature of our being and in the process we may well discover that many more illnesses are caused by our own attitude of mind. But suffering is not as simple as that. It is those who do not suffer who might well ask, 'Why are we not suffering?' If Christ suffers along with suffering humanity, there is no reason why we should find ourselves excluded. Suffering caused by broken relationships or mental attitudes can be as bad as physical suffering.

When we look into the eyes of suffering people we are looking into the eyes of Christ. That is why caring is a worthy Christian vocation – as we serve the sick, the dying, the homeless, the starving, the refugees, we are helping in the healing work of Christ and also ministering to him. I have always taken great comfort in the words of St Francis de Sales to someone who was sick:

> While I think of you sick and suffering in your bed I regard you with special reverence and honour and one who is God's own child, clothed with his robe, visited by his own hand. When our Lord was on the Cross he was proclaimed King, even by his enemies, and those souls whom he raises to the Cross reign with him there.

We may never wish suffering on others, or do anything to inflict it, but in the presence of suffering we are very close to our crucified Lord. There we may listen to him as he speaks of the agonies of suffering. He speaks to us through the AIDS victim, the starving, and those who suffer from personal or institutional violence. Ministering to those who suffer is an act of worship. Our inspiration is the Cross.

We have still not reached the heart of the matter. There are plenty of people who suffer for no good reason. What about the young child who dies of leukaemia, the inno- cent victim of a road accident, the agonies of those who suffer as a result of flood, earthquake or lightning? Is the implication that some people are too good to go on living? We hear echoes of remarks like this in the words of the Psalmist when he implies that God allows the evil to thrive. There is, however, another side to this. The good who suffer often do so in a creative way. I knew a twenty-two-year-old man who knew he was dying of leu- kaemia, but he did so with great dignity. He absorbed all the bitterness, resentment and anger which might, not unreasonably, have been his response. It was good to be with him, and as he died he cared more for those he left behind than for himself. The very acceptance of that suffering was a transformation, not only for him, but for those around him. This is not to deny the forces of evil but to overcome them. That is what we see on the Cross. God is the Creator who made all things. God, who gave us the freedom to love and to hate, takes the responsibility for the world he has made. We can blame God for the evil in the world. On the Cross we see God taking it all upon himself. 'Yes,' he seems to be saying, 'I am respons- ible,' but in such a way as to stem the violence and trans- form it, not to spread it further.

Against this background we need to hear the words of Jesus: 'Turn the other cheek', 'Go the extra mile', 'Give to him who asks'. Only in this way can hate be trans- formed into love and violence be turned into acceptance. The violent man expects you to hit back – he does not know what to do when you do not. To love your enemy is to change both him and you. Such idealism in Christianity is often attacked as unrealistic. Certainly it presents some very deep dilemmas. Those who have advocated passive resistance, like Ghandi and Martin Luther King, have often indirectly provoked considerable violence as a result. They have been killed in the process of their passive resistance.

'Nowhere in the Bible,' says the 'Kairos Document', 'has it ever been suggested that we ought to try and reconcile good and evil, God and the devil.' We are called to do away with evil, injustice, oppression and sin, not to come to terms with it. But how?

No one who was aware of the tyrannies of Hitler can really reject the argument of a just war. It was Dietrich Bonhoeffer who expressed it in the analogy that if the car driver was driving the car over a cliff the best thing to do would be to push him out. It was a tragedy that the Allies took so little interest in those planning Hitler's assassination. The Second World War could have finished much earlier. The doctrine of just war imposes very severe restrictions on how war may be conducted: the indiscriminate bombing of civilians, the total obliteration as a result of nuclear war are clearly morally wrong. Churchmen such as Bishop George Bell, who spoke out against such tactics, suffered badly at the hands of the British Government. Even in war our actions need to be determined by the Gospel and not by what is purely expedient – and that is not easy.

If a just war is conceded as a possibility, then just revolution must be conceded as well. Churches around the world can be found resisting unjust governments in many ways. The freedom of speech and worship has to be preserved. The economic boycott of white shops in South Africa was a powerful weapon towards change. Much can be done without recourse to violence, even when those seeking to preserve the status quo resort to violence.

We have to look at root causes and not just at the effects. The root causes of injustice in the world lie in the greed of the West; it lies in the unjust distribution of this world's goods; it is revealed in the exploitation of poor people by multinational companies; it lies in the exploitation of the natural environment by the breaking down of the ozone layer, the removal of rain forests and the pollution of seas and rivers; it lies in the immoral export of weapons and arms in order to boost the Western economy. While it may be morally justified for a country to have an arms trade of a limited sort to preserve its own peace, there can be no justification for exporting arms to other countries where the build up of weapons almost inevitably leads either to oppression or war.

We are just beginning to see that if we are to end violence, exploitation and oppression it is going to require a very radical change of lifestyle by every person, not least in the Western world. We are beginning to see that one way to overcome evil is by simpler living. This is the great cause which the Church needs to espouse at this time. Simple living brings together many things which the Christian Gospel stands for. The description of the life of the Early Church in the second chapter of Acts gives us a model of fellowship, of sharing, of living together in a community of love and acceptance. We see how the issues which we usually sum up under the term 'Spirituality' actually spill over into our daily living and have economic, social and political implications.

A further way of removing the causes of violence, oppression and suspicion lies in very great efforts at mutual understanding. This means understanding other faiths. This is often called 'dialogue'. We live in a world where the conflicts between other faiths are reaching disturbing proportions. We cannot ignore the existence of other world religions in our midst and if we are concerned with the wholeness of God's world we have to see ways of understanding, sharing, supporting and strengthening each other. The whole question of relationships with other faiths is a vast matter. All I wish to assert here is that if we relate to other faiths we have to do so on the

basis of the principle which we find in the Gospel. We
cannot use methods which are contrary to or unworthy
of the Gospel. It is clear from an analysis of religious
dialogue what these principles are.

1. We approach each other on the basis of our shared
    humanity. We should want to share our values and
    understandings with each other, thus to begin with we
    may not be discussing distinctively religious matters at
    all.

2. We need to understand ourselves very well. The better
    we grasp the meaning and practice of our own faith,
    the more we shall be able to share. This means also
    publicly admitting our faults and failings in not living
    up to the faith we profess.

3. We have to do our best to enter into the position of
    the people we are talking to – for instance, in Christ-
    ian-Islamic dialogue it is vital that Christians read the
    Koran and Muslims read the Bible. For some it may
    well mean going to live in an alien culture and
    experiencing it for a long time.

4. We have to find ways of speaking a common language.
    This can only come out of careful listening to each
    other.

5. Nothing will happen unless we are honest and open
    with each other, for honesty itself will communicate
    truth.

6. It is no use entering into dialogue unless we are
    ourselves willing to change. God will be speaking to
    us through those we encounter.

7. There must be attempts not just to talk together but
    to act together and share in the common tasks of
    helping suffering humanity. In this way we can grow
    together in compassion.

8. We need to share and understand each other's ways

of prayer and worship. We can gain much mutual enrichment in this way.

The way of dialogue is not just a task of understanding, but is itself a proper form of spiritual discipline. All the points listed above are applicable not just to dialogue but to all our daily living. Again spirituality permeates the whole of our being.

If we really are concerned about suffering in the world and if we wish to share in Christ's redemptive work, we have to become the community of the Crucified. This will require much from us. First of all, it means doing what we can to remove avoidable pain and suffering wherever possible. This begins with our own lifestyle.

Secondly, it means seeking to establish communities of understanding so that the causes of violence and conflict may be revealed.

Thirdly, it means reaching out in care and concern for all the suffering and treating them all with the reverence due to the Christ who suffers in them.

Finally, it means realising that those who choose this path of love and self-sacrifice are very likely to threaten and stir up deep anger and violence against themselves by so doing. We can see this in the lives of the martyrs. We see it supremely in Jesus himself. Only so can evil be transformed into good and God's love finally be made known.

Passion of Christ my comfort be.

We shall need all the strength that God can give us. Very truly did Dietrich Bonhoeffer say, 'When Jesus calls a man, he bids him come and die.'

6

O Good Jesu listen to me

Taylor Caldwell in her novel *The Man Who Listens* described a place where people could go to speak to the Man Who Listens. It was simply a room into which people went and talked. No one ever saw the Man. When the inner room was entered it simply contained a crucifix. People felt the security to talk, to unburden themselves and to discover solutions to their problems. The art of listening is vitally needed in today's world. Some people pay large amounts of money to go to a psychiatrist, others find a friend, a priest, and even in the context of a family we can find a listening ear. Yet our world is one of so much noise, that our ears are distracted by words, music and industrial sound the whole time, with the result that the art of listening is becoming too rare. It is only too easy to listen to someone with half an ear and only hear half of what is being said. Real listening requires one's full attention and can be very demanding.

Our prayer is an invitation to God to listen to us as we pour out our feelings and emotions. Yet if the biblical analogy of forgiveness is right – that God forgives those who forgive others – so God listens to those who listen to others. It is not only time and space for God which we need to find, it is time and space for other people. Part of our spiritual discipline means learning the art of avail-ability to others. I have only met this in a few people. Very often clergy are the worst: they are so busy justifying their existence that they are not available. I know one bishop who, if you asked to see him, would get his secretary to make you a booking for three weeks hence. I knew another bishop of a very large diocese who, when I asked if I could see him, said, 'Yes, come now'. Being that available is a great art, but it can be done. It is partly the art of diary management so that written into it is space for the crises and the emergencies. Behind it is an attitude of mind which does not seek to fill every moment of the day with activity. One of the causes of the breakdown of family life has been the attitude instilled in contemporary Britain that we must work hard all the time to achieve success. We witness many homes where the father is a shadowy figure, commuting many miles, leaving for work early and arriving home very late, and this is matched by hard-pressed mothers, often themselves working part-time to keep up high mortgage payments. No time, no space is set apart for family living; the result is the breakdown of relationships.

Living needs space – space to be. The solitary life may be the vocation of very few, but the capacity to know how to be alone and find space to be alone is a vital part of mature living. If we cannot come to terms with ourselves, how can we possibly help others? One of the powerful passages in Bonhoeffer's *Life Together* is his chapter entitled 'The Day Alone'. It begins with these words: 'Many people seek fellowship because they are afraid to be alone. Because they cannot stand loneliness they are driven to seek the company of other people.'

He warns against people using the Church as a means of diversion from facing their own problems, and he produces a very important adage: 'Let him who cannot be alone beware of community. Let him who is not in community beware of being alone.' He makes an important distinction between *loneliness*, which is a sense of being lost and unloved, and *aloneness*, which is an assertion of individuality in relation to community. Bonhoeffer then goes on to describe the need for meditation, prayer and intercession as part of the function of our solitude. The real test of both the community and the individual is how they relate to each other. A person who cannot cope with aloneness has nothing to give to the community. The community which makes someone weak and dependent has failed to be a real community. We need the blessing both of being solitary and of being in community. Both, says Bonhoeffer, are dependent upon the Word of God which is addressed to the individual and the community.

If we are to be listening people who can help others, we need to have been listened to. We have to learn how to give ourselves to others in such a way that they know they are being taken seriously.

A prayer in the *Ancrene Riwle* refers to Christ abiding in us. Perhaps that is another way of looking at this matter. When we listen to others, it is Christ listening to them through us. Prayer is all part of a massive conversation that God is having with himself in the Trinity. I find this a powerful image, for the whole of life is lived and sustained in God. He abides in us and we abide in him. This is an image which St John spells out very fully in his Gospel, beginning with the call to the first disciples. It relates not only to prayer but also to our mission in the world. In the first chapter of St John's Gospel, after John the Baptist has pointed out to two disciples of his that Jesus is the Lamb of God, they follow him. They ask him where he is staying and he replies, 'Come and see'. 'So,' St John continues, 'they went and saw where he was staying and spent the rest of the day with him' (John 1:35–39). Here we see the beginning of that great Johannine theme summed up later in the Gospel: 'Dwell in Me as I in you' (John 15:4). The two disciples followed Jesus and abode with him. Before Jesus can go out in mission he has to gather a community around him. 'Come and see,' says Jesus. This is an invitation to every one of us to seek the mysteries of faith and to be in the presence of Jesus. It means being willing to cross new frontiers: in order for us to discover new things, we shall find we do not have all the answers. Jesus is always going before us

– we do need to abide in him to find out who we are and where he is taking us. The space to be alone is vital.

Anthony Storr, in his book *Solitude*, analyses the importance of being alone. It is from solitude that many people learn to be creative. We live, he says, in a society which thinks that many of our problems can be resolved through personal relationships. This is a fallacy: solitude can be very creative. Anthony Storr examines this through people who had to face solitary confinement, or were alone through deprivation as children or through bereavement. He shows that through being forced back on ourselves we can find hidden resources. Lonely children, like Beatrix Potter, create imaginary worlds which become the basis of wonderful books. Beethoven's deafness enhanced his music. Those whose minds have been regularly stimulated by reading, prayer and intellectual activity find it easier to cope with solitary confinement. A more creative society would undoubtedly appear if people were not so afraid of being alone.

There has been a long tradition in the Church of going on retreat. At this present time Christian retreat houses and religious houses are hard-pressed by people wishing to come on retreat. The retreatant has the advantage of being alone in an ordered manner. Meals are provided, a framework of worship and addresses are available. There is even someone to listen to you, should you need it. Here is a way of abiding in Christ which is readily available to many. There are three other forms of retreat which can also be used. The first is the solitary retreat, where one joins in the life of a religious community, but is left to one's own devices. This would be no way to start, but for those experienced in retreats, it can be a growing point. Some people find the presence of other people on retreat a hindrance.

The second, which is very fashionable at the moment, is the long 'one to one' retreat. This is often based on the Ignatian methods and the retreatant has a regular meeting with an individual conductor in order to direct the retreat in the way he or she could go. Such retreats require very great skill on the part of the conductor. It is vital that the conductor does not impose his or her own views on the retreatant but enables the individual to develop in his or her own way. It is a method open to dangerous manipulation in the wrong hands and a degree of confidence is needed on all sides. The retreatant needs to be strong, open and aware of what is happening. The conductor needs to be highly sensitive and very skilled in personal counselling to ensure that the relationship is creative and not destructive.

The third approach, which can be related to the others, is the retreat taken at home. This may best be done in a parish where several people decide to go through the exercise together. They may attend church for daily worship, but fit the rest of their extra times of prayer around their ordinary living. An admirable time to do this would be in Holy Week when the Church's Liturgy provides a great deal of material which may be used as material for meditation. Address, Maundy Thursday Vigil, Good Friday Liturgy, Three Hours Devotion and the Easter Vigil can provide a framework which is almost too rich. One of the easiest ways of making a retreat could well be in a parish, living at home but using the Holy Week Liturgy as a basis for it. Groups of parishioners sharing such an exercise would enrich themselves and the life of the parish. It would be good for them to meet and share their experiences at the end of it.

O Good Jesu listen to me.

There has, particularly in the Eastern Church, been a tradition of saying the 'Jesus Prayer'. This is a simple, effective form of prayer whereby the person repeats the words, 'Lord Jesus Christ have mercy upon me a sinner,' or simply the word 'Jesus'. Here is a way of fixing our mind on God and his redemptive love which can become as much part of our life as our daily eating. In an age of much hustle and busyness, such a simple recollection can link our daily living with our more specific times of prayer.

We call on the name of Jesus, that name which means Saviour. It is the same name as Joshua – he who led Israel into the Promised Land; he who went before to show the way. It is an image taken up very fully in the Epistle to the Hebrews, where Jesus is seen as our forerunner, blazing the trail to open the way of redemption and liberation for his people. Jesus is he who stands alone, who is crucified outside the camp. We are called to go to him, to be alone where he is alone. This is the Jesus we call upon: he who went apart into a desert place to be tempted; he who rose early to pray on his own; he who agonised alone in the Garden of Gethsemane while his followers slept; he who died alone on the Cross crying out, 'My God, my God, why have you forsaken me'. If we cannot face aloneness we certainly cannot follow our Lord.

O Good Jesu listen to me.

7

In thy wounds I fain would hide

John Wesley's metrical version of the *Anima Christi* has a close partner in Toplady's hymn 'Rock of Ages':

> Rock of ages, cleft for me,
> let me hide myself in thee;
> let the water and the blood,
> from thy riven side which flowed,
> Be of sin the double cure:
> Cleanse me from its guilt and power.

Wesley follows the Johannine pattern of 'abiding', 'close sheltered in thy bleeding side'; Toplady simply talks of 'hiding'. But what does this hiding in Christ mean? If, as we have seen, we need to share in suffering humanity, is the hiding a way of escape? Is this hiding a call to the solitary life where we can escape the agonies of the world around us? Too often we interpret it that way and how easily we sing the words of that other hymn, 'Jesu, lover of my soul':

> Hide me, O my Saviour, hide,
> till the storm of life is past;
> safe unto the haven guide,
> O receive my soul at last.

That is a form of escapism. Hiding in Christ to avoid the problems of living cannot be a Christian way. Religion is not a drug to be used to escape from the responsibilities of life. The reverse is the reality. We hide in Christ to face the reality, the suffering and the pain in him and with him.

In thy wounds I fain would hide.

Surely the biblical text which lies behind this is that of St Paul in his letter to the Colossians: 'You died and now your life lies hidden with Christ in God' (Colossians 3:3). Paul calls his fellow Christians to enter into the mind of Christ. Their thoughts are to dwell in Christ's death and to die with him. Instead of being buried in the earth at death they are to be buried with Christ in his new life.

This is the hidden life. This is the secret discipline. We are to pray in secret: we are not to show our acts of devotion to be seen of men (Matthew 6:1–18). The secret place which we enter is the wound of Christ, where, cleansed and redeemed, we may find new life. From the secret discipline there emerges a growing and changing relationship in ourselves and within the Christian community.

It was the early, persecuted Church, worshipping in the catacombs, who first practised the secret discipline (*Disciplina Arcana*). There they prayed together; there they entered into the sacramental life of Baptism and Eucharist. Their activities were misunderstood as being subversive, but they had the strength to live out their faith.

Dietrich Bonhoeffer called for the Church to find a 'non-religious interpretation of Christianity'. If the Gospel was to become known to modern secular man it had to find a new language – a language which was not dependent on the old religious categories. It had, moreover, to be a faith which lay at the heart of life, a faith which incorporated every aspect of being. It was no use, he thought, to propound a 'god of the gaps' theology, where God was simply the explanation for what we did not understand. As Dean Inge put it years earlier: 'Those who take refuge in gaps are liable to find themselves in a tight corner when the gaps begin to close'. The non-religious interpretation could only come about if at its heart lay the secret discipline. A world affirming faith would only emerge out of a discipline where the central truths of faith were guarded and sustained within the Christian community. This is well expressed by Eberhard Bethge in his biography of Bonhoeffer when he points out that Bonhoeffer saw an intimate connection between his idea of worldliness and a non-religious interpretation of Christianity and the secret discipline. He did not see how you could have the one without the other. Many critics of Bonhoeffer have not understood this.

It is this balance which this book is trying to explore. The balance is uncomfortable because we are always being called back from the one to the other. We can only affirm the world by being hidden in Christ. We can only find Christ by affirming the world. Life is not divided: the Creator is also the Redeemer.

We dare not hide to escape. We must hide in order to be bold and make experiments in the effective communication of the Gospel. It is possible that it is at this very point that the attempts to proclaim a Gospel relevant to secular man have gone so wrong this century. We should not denigrate the attempts of modern theologians to make such connections. Is it that they did not take seriously enough the secret discipline? Did they realise the way the discipline keeps the links with the past? It is a delicate balance. The desire to communicate the Gospel in modern terms has to be balanced by living and praying within the tradition. This is where Bonhoeffer is such a significant figure. His lectures on pastoral care and his reflections on community living go alongside the need to communicate the Gospel to 'Man Come of Age'. The one enables the other. This is because Bonhoeffer sees life whole – he realises that the pastor cannot effectively care unless his life is one of prayer: 'Other people must know that I stand before God as I stand before them. I depend upon the guidance of the Holy Spirit.'

Thus whether it is in communicating the faith, pastoral care or plain daily living, the discipline is needed so that, in Paul's words, 'It is no longer I that live but Christ lives in me' (Galatians 2:20).

The Christian life, like the Cross itself, is a death to self. It is a way of death to personal plans, personal ambition and selfish desires. It is a hidden life which is not lived out of the world, but in the midst of the world for Christ's sake.

This is a very hard path for people trapped in the culture of our own age. Our world is brought up on the language of self-fulfilment, of avoidance of repression and the need for personal satisfaction. It is a consumer's world where everyone tells us we should have what we want. In political terms – either of the Right or the Left – we face ideologies which hold that everything is determined by economic factors. We are encouraged to think that competition is a good thing and that all that really matters is effective productivity. This is not the hidden life of Christ. How easy it is to accept the culture around us and consecrate it into the Church. We are told by proponents of the Church Growth Movement that the effective preaching of the Gospel will be richly blessed by large congregations. We are told that a lot of marketing techniques suitably adapted will enable us to be 'effective and successful clergy'. We are encouraged to reduce the Gospel to simple, banal songs which anyone can sing. We are told to look for signs and wonders, like people of the mediaeval world, as a sure proof of God's activity among us. We are told that faith is about prayers being answered and that the man of God will be successful in business. We are told that prayer is an important part of our own self-fulfilment.

We have not so learned Christ. Remember the terrible words of Dean Inge: 'We hear of empty churches, I know of churches which would be far emptier if the Gospel was preached in them.'

The Gospel tells us that whoever would save his life

must lose it. In love everything must be given, nothing retained. The hidden, secret discipline runs counter to much in our modern world. We have to die to Christ. That is what our Baptism is about. Fr Benson often used to remind people that the risen Christ appeared, 'When the doors were shut'. There is a secret life which is also a form of protest against much in modern society.

The great agonies of trying to seek the unity of Christian people is another illustration of this. The failure to achieve unity lies in a failure to live out the Gospel. Jesus says, 'Whosoever would save his life will lose it' (Matthew 10:39). The ecumenical challenge to the churches is to die to their own separate identity and live to God in a greater unity. The call to the churches is to take a leap of faith and not cling to what we know; we have to let go and discover something more. The continued separation of the churches is a sure sign of their own failure to live out the Gospel they proclaim. This has a stultifying effect on all attempts to communicate the Gospel to others. Ecumenical spirituality (the common living out by Christians of the shared discipline of prayer and worship) is one way in which this will be broken down. The great vision of the Abbe Couturier of 'the invisible monastery' where we become united in prayer through our unity in God is something we need to rediscover. Perhaps the time has come for the church leaders to call all Christian people to a basic personal discipline of prayer and worship which would bind us all together and deepen our commitment. New ecumenical structures will avail nothing if the churches do not surrender autonomy to give them authority. They will also avail nothing if there does not lie behind them a hidden discipline which lives out of the great Christian tradition and works out its relationship with life today.

The power of the Gospel lies in the secret discipline. It is this power which enables martyrs to stand firm. It is this power which enables Christians to stand against the tendencies of society and have different priorities to those around them. This hiddenness is for the life of the world. It is so because it has the Cross at its centre. God turns the values of this world upside down. Bonhoeffer sums up the power of the saints like this:

> There is one place and only one place, where the poorest, meekest and most sorely tried of men is to be found – on the Cross of Golgotha. The community which is the subject of the beatitudes is the community of the crucified. With him it has lost all and with him it has found all. It is the Cross which makes the beatitudes possible.
>
> These meek strangers are bound to provoke the world to insult, violence and slander. Too menacing, too loud are the voices of these poor meek men, too patient and too silent their suffering. Too powerful are the testimony of their poverty and their endurance of the wrongs which the world inflicts upon them.

In thy wounds I fain would hide.

8

Ne'er to be parted from thy side

Many have yearned for a total awareness of God. Can that be possible in this life? Certainly no one can live perpetually in a high state of contemplation. To be aware of God is not the same thing as living in the presence of God: that is something we cannot avoid whether we are aware of it or not. The philosophers talk of the unknowability of the constant. We are not aware of the world going round because it always is. The presence of God is much the same, but that is not to say that we can afford to ignore the fact. Allowing ourselves to be reminded of the presence of God is desirable.

How do we go about it? It was Brother Lawrence's *Practice of the Presence of God* which led many people to seek God in the ordinary, not just in the spiritual. A similar point is well made in the Rule of St Benedict when he writes that the vessels in the kitchen are to be treated as if they were the vessels for the Eucharist on the altar. It was Jean-Pierre de Caussade, the seventeenth-century Jesuit, who grappled with this problem in his book *Self Abandonment to the Divine Providence.* Caussade was in a way an existentialist. We are doing what God wants us to do; every moment is a challenge to serve God. *Now* is God's moment.

There are two strands in the history of Christian spirituality. They are the way of negation and the way of affirmation. The way of negation says, 'Deny yourself, remove all hindrances on the way to God'. We have seen that an element of this is essential. The way of affirmation says,

'Do this, seek God, this is God's world. Use everything to relate to God'. Such a way was proposed by Jean-Pierre de Caussade. Apart from his main work, *Self Abandonment to the Divine Providence*, his writings consist of a book entitled *On Prayer*, which is written in dialogue form, and a vast collection of letters written chiefly to nuns.

His basic assumption is that God rules over everything and is always active in the world. Faith enbles us to see the divine action in every part of life. To see the divine action in everything is the way to affirmative living. The secret of living is to surrender everything to the will of God. It is not so much what we do that matters, but that we surrender our will. So he prays:

> Lord I wish nothing but Thy holy will. Prayer, action, vocal or mental prayers, inactivity or silence, in faith or in light, lost in thy general grace, or precisely and specifically distinct, all distractions, Lord, are nothing; for it is Thy will that makes the real and one and only virtue of them all.

This being the case, how do we find God's will? There is, says de Caussade, 'The sacrament of the present moment': 'At every occurrence we should say, "It is the Lord"; and in all circumstances we should find a gift from God.' We surrender our will to God at each moment. That is true humility. Life does not work out the way we wanted it to – so what? Whatever happens is what God wants. It all sounds very simple. For nuns living in a religious community it may well have been – their life was already very circumscribed. If we followed this too literally we could be acquiescing in all sorts of injustices and seeing God not just as loving but also as very unfair. At the same time de Caussade is right in seeing the challenge of God and of the Gospel in everything which happens. Faith and the world have to hang together: 'What instructs us is what happens to us from moment to moment; that is what forms us in the experimental science which Jesus Christ willed to acquire.' He points out that if we knew we were meeting a King in disguise we would behave very differently than if we did not know he was a King.

While not going all the way with de Caussade, we can affirm that in every moment there is a challenge from God. We may have to denounce or reject what we encounter, we may be pressed to new activity by what someone says to us. In each moment there is the need for a response. This enables us to forget ourselves and seek to serve God in others, so we can be aware of God in all that happens.

De Caussade had the pastoral care of nuns. It has been suggested that he used his authority to dominate women and put them in a position of subjection. His use of the Annunciation as a symbol of abandonment can be interpreted as a form of subjugation. This is a serious danger, but it is not implicit in the principles which he is expounding.

Bishop Jeremy Taylor, a chaplain to King Charles I, is someone else who reflects on this matter. In his *Holy Living and Holy Dying* he talks about the practice of the presence of God. He begins with the same point as de Caussade. God is present at all times and even understands every thought. He lists the presence of God in six ways: God is present by his very essence but never limited, because he is infinite. God is present by his power; he develops everything in Creation. God is present in some spaces in a more special manner to manifest himself for extraordinary purposes. God is especially present in holy places and where worship is taking place. God is present in the hearts of his people by the Holy Spirit. God is present in the consciences of all people, whether good or bad. He argues that we are called always to act as if we are in the presence of God.

He suggests various acts of prayer to make this real. We can recollect the words of the Psalmist: 'Where can I escape from your Spirit, where flee from your presence? If I climb up to heaven you are there. If I make my bed in Sheol, you are there' (Psalm 139:7–8). We should begin all prayer with an act of adoration reminding us of his presence. We should look at all aspects of the world as revealing the power of God. We should also offer up acts of prayer throughout the day. We should remember God is present in our neighbours and also in every creature so that we should respect all animals as part of his glory.

One thing is clear in that seeking the presence of God must affirm the totality of being. Nothing is outside the sphere of God's concern. All life is what spirituality is about. The liberation theologians of Latin America have seen this very clearly. Gustavo Guiteirrez defines spirituality as a way of living according to the Spirit. It is an affirmation and a choice within the whole of life, thus it is 'an over all comprehensive attitude'. For him this means the choice of living with the poor and experiencing, not just occasionally but for every moment of the day, the deprivations, injustices and hardships of the life of the poor. That is where Jesus is found. Spirituality is about the totality of living, revealed in the total giving of oneself to the community in which one is placed.

Many more could feel a vocation to serve the poor, but it is not the way for all. Jesus was 'a gluttonous man and a wine bibber' (Matthew 11:19; Luke 7:34), and there are those who will have to give themselves to other societies and cultures, to the rich and powerful, where they are open to all forms of coercion and self-indulgence – but these people, too, need to learn of the Kingdom. Once we perceive that our faith is part of our total living, we will see that we can never be separated from the Lord, for we find him in every moment of being.

The conservation of time, therefore, is important. The space set aside for prayer and worship is what enables us to find God in the whole of life. Entering into the round of the daily worship of the Church is one way; the pattern of prayer we choose can be another. At no time can we neglect to find the space which enables us to recall the acts, the acceptance, the love of God and bring them into our life.

It is not a matter of being holy, but of living the whole of our life with the whole of our being and discovering that God has already given himself to us.

III   UNION

9

Guard me, should the foe assail me

The *Anima Christi* seems to have been used as a sort of defence against the devil. Mediaeval man had a profound belief in a real devil who tempted people, fought to win them into his power and to torment them in hell. The world was a battle ground: there was heaven above and hell beneath, and devils and demons fought for the souls of people. Signs of the devil's activity were seen all around. The devil threw a stone at St Wulfstan of Worcester while he prayed (in other words a stone fell out of the church roof); there were witches to be tried. Life was black and white: the devil had to be thrown down.

The makers of horror films still prey on our collective memory of a world like this, but very few people really believe in it. We seem to be facing some sort of resurgence of interest in Satanism. It seems on one side to be a way of trying to justify some horrible forms of sexual abuse. On the other side it seems to be being promoted by fundamentalist Christians who wish to prove the power and existence of the devil so that they can encourage people to return to the world view of the New Testament and to reject a more scientific, post-enlightenment viewpoint. In so doing they are being dishonest and destructive – dishonest because this is not a world view that a thinking person can seriously accept (they are thereby making it an obstacle to evangelism); destructive because it produces a hidden connivance with the child sexual abusers who need such a camouflage to justify their own cruel and disturbed practices.

There is no need for belief in a personal devil by Christian people today. Belief in the devil becomes a very convenient way of avoiding personal responsibility. When something goes wrong, or we act in a wrong way, we can blame the devil (and seek exorcism) rather than admit our own failures and failings. The concept of the devil has now also been superseded by a much greater understanding of various forms of mental illness like paranoia and schizophrenia. The literature of Satanism and witchcraft can be analysed to fit into categories now well known to the psychiatrist. Psychiatric treatment is often the answer.

There are very difficult questions which are raised about how the Church responds to people who feel possessed, haunted or have been caught up in undesirable practices. The mediaeval Church had a whole system of exorcism to deal with such matters. Do we ignore that altogether? Or are there insights which can be useful?

There has been a growing interest in such matters within the Church in recent years. Within the Church of England there is now a whole network of Bishops' Advisors in exorcism. The need has arisen because of a considerable number of people turning to the Church for help of this nature. The whole area of the psychic is a complex one.

At one level we need to ask why our society is becoming one where so many abnormal patterns of behaviour are arising. The break-up of family life is clearly a factor in this, the development of a drug subculture is another. There is still a great deal of folklore embedded in our society – the popularity of astrologers is an example of this.

Alongside this we have to face the fact that there are whole areas of the human mind and human behaviour about which we still know very little. Few these days would question the reality of telepathy. People often seem to be able to communicate without words and at a distance. The growing interest in psychosomatic medicine and alternative forms of healing which acknowledge the effect of the mind on the body (and vice versa) shows that we have within ourselves powers of healing which often lie dormant. The analysis of religious experience which Professor Alistair Hardy initiated in Oxford is another area which is revealing whole layers of experience which have been rarely expressed and hardly examined. Alongside the exploration of outer space, the human race seems to be on the brink of an exploration of inner space which is going to reveal a great deal more about human nature.

How we interpret such phenomena is a matter of the greatest importance. The fact that some people are healed by the laying on of hands is not necessarily a proof that someone is a healer or that it is a direct (rather than a general) intervention by God. The fact that people see ghosts or find themselves feeling possessed by an evil spirit is not a proof of the existence of another world or of the reality of the devil. We are here moving into deep psychological areas. A group of people may convince others that their own world view is the right one and interpret many events through their own perspective. The fact that a group of people agree with each other does not mean that what they perceive is objectively the case. Total objectivity is not possible. The whole phenomena of new religious movements or of New Age faiths show us how easy it is for people to be brainwashed into a way of thinking. Dr William Sergeant in his important book *Battle for the Mind* revealed how much of this can be done. It would be very easy for the Church to become just another ghetto of like-minded, brainwashed people – that is why it is so vital that we assert great diversity in the Church and welcome many strands of tradition together. The 'Friends of God' were presumably such a group. Their visions, conversions and other experiences fit into the same sort of pattern as some New Age groups.

Should the Church be involved in exorcism, especially if it finds the existence of a personal devil no longer part of its agenda? This is not an easy question. When people cry for help they have to be met where they are. If someone thinks his house is haunted it is no use the vicar going along and saying, 'It's all right, there is no such thing as a ghost'. At the same time, to go along with holy water and bell, book and candle may well mean that the priest is conniving in a situation which needs resolving by love, psychotherapy and the healing of relationships. Much caution is needed. Some old prayers may help; the celebration of the Eucharist in the house may help; a simple laying on of hands may bring peace as a way to further contact and involvement; simple prayer may be used – the *Anima Christi* might be such a prayer.

If we reject a personal devil, that is not the same thing as rejecting the existence of evil in our world. We have seen the evil of tyrannical regimes; the grave damage caused by the threat of nuclear war; the evil effect on the Third World of the greed of modern Western society. We see in our streets the evil of our greed and the suppression of the poor. We see the evil effects of unjust legislation in homelessness and famine. We witness the evil effect of the breakdown of family life. We read in our paper of the exploitation of children in slave labour and child prostitution. We hear too frequently of the evils of torture and effects of sexual perversion and drug abuse. There is evil to be overcome. There are foes to be guarded against. It is a part of our whole spirituality to denounce evil, and we cannot start without acknowledging our own contribution to the evil in the world. We all need new forms of self-examination which help us to see how we participate in evil: we live in a country which has boosted its economy by massive arms sales to other countries; we live in a world where our treatment of the natural order is leading to its destruction; we all have experiences of broken relationships in our own lives which are part of the general breakdown we see around us. There is much need for repentance.

We have to share with others ways in which society may be changed. There will be no black and white solutions. We shall be forced into political action. We shall need to judge all political parties to see how far they are caring for the environment, supporting the poor and the oppressed, bringing justice to the Third World, combatting racism and improving education and literacy. That is not enough either, for we then need to realise that there will be a price to pay to enable such things to happen and the price will be very high. I am not an economist, but I cannot see how we may find a fairer world without the people of the Western economic powers being willing to sacrifice aspects of their affluence rather than just exporting them. Much of Western life is too undesirable to be exported at all. Politicians on the whole appeal to people's greed, to their acquisitiveness, to their desire to have a higher standard of living. Perhaps in the ecological debate we may be seeing a way out of this – people may just be beginning to see that such things are not in their best interests. What will it profit a man if he gains the whole world and loses his soul? What will it profit us if we live in affluence which is destroying the whole hemisphere?

Christians must be called to fight against evil – they must fight only with the weapons of the Cross. They will have to find ways of appealing to people's desire for love and self-surrender, for the need to give rather than take. The world, and the politicians, will ridicule us for that. There may be just enough signs in today's world to show that it is not a completely impossible dream, but the price will be high. Evil will do its best to resist it.

Fr Sobrino makes it clear that there is no spirituality which does not involve political action on behalf of and with the poor. There is another means of fighting evil which many people do not take into account. It relates to our thinking; it relates to the act that we all interact with each other. St Paul gives us the clue when he writes: 'All that is true, all that is noble, all that is just and pure, all that is lovable and attractive, whatever is excellent and admirable – fill your thoughts with these things' (Philippians 4:8).

It is part of the point of prayer and meditation. We need to be steeped in the signs, the symbolism, the ethos

of the things of God and so take our part in the rejec-
tion of evil. My thoughts are not solely my thoughts –
they affect the way other people think. If I fill my mind
with violence, pornography, greed and love of money,
even if it is only ideas, that increases the amount of such
thinking in the world. This is not something to be tri-
umphalist about – that is why Clean Up campaigns are so
ineffective. We all need to be aware that what we are
thinking about affects other people. There is a level of
awareness of sin here which is far from common. People
often say that what people do or think in private is their
own affair. It is not: it affects the rest of us. It is like the
argument which says that people can do what they like
with their own money, that people can choose private
education or medicine, or choose all sorts of things for
themselves. It might be true in a world of unlimited
resources, but it is not true in our world. Private medicine
and education inevitably reduce the availability of good
staff and equipment for the public sector. My choices, my
thinking, affect the choices of others. We may not be able
to limit these choices, but we should be making people
aware of the effect of what they are doing. This may all
seem very idealistic, but our minds are the vital part of
our being. What we think affects all of us: either we can
choose to increase the good in the world by our thinking
or diminish it.

Mind of Christ sanctify me.

We can go beyond thinking. We are affected deeply by
sounds, symbols and senses. There is a whole question
here about the role of music and the arts within our total
spirituality. People need not only to think of the beauty
but to see it, hear it, sense it around them. New worlds
can be opened up. Glimpses of God can come from the
work of writers, musicians, artists, poets. How far are we
all giving beauty to the world? This way we can cast out
evil.

10

Call me when my life shall fail me

In the Neueminsterkirche in the town of Wurzburg in Bavaria, there is a very unusual crucifix. Ever since I saw it the image has stayed with me. The crucified Christ is on the Cross. He has a crown of thorns on his head, there is an open wound in his side. He has nails through his hands but his arms are not stretched out on the Cross. They are in a cradling position, like a mother holding a baby in her arms. There is very deep power in this image. If the outstretched arms of Christ symbolise God's embrace and acceptance of humanity, the cradling arms symbolise supporting, loving care. This is the mother Christ. It is an affirmation of the feminine in the God-head. This is an accepted theme in mediaeval mystical theology. Dame Julian of Norwich talks about God as mother: 'Our Saviour is our true mother, in whom we are endlessly born and out of whom we shall never come.'

The Wurzburg crucifix is in a sense a meditation on such a text. Julian's writings are fully trinitarian in their understanding of God's love.

The second person of the Trinity is our mother in nature in our substantial creation in whom we are founded and rooted, and he is our mother of mercy in taking our sensuality . . . and by the power of his passion, his death and his resurrection he unites us to his substance.

A comparison is given between the pangs of childbirth and the pains, suffering and blood-letting on the Cross.

Moreover, Christ our mother feeds us. Some mediaeval writers compared the wounds of Christ with a mother's breast. The wounds of Christ bringing forth blood and water are our nourishment: this we find in the sacraments. Grace Janzten points out that mediaeval medical theory believed the milk coming from a mother's breasts was processed blood. Milk and blood become interchangeable, so Julian can link the Passion with the Eucharist through the image of motherhood:

> The mother can give her child to suck her milk, but our precious mother Jesus can feed us with himself, and does, most courteously and most tenderly, with the blessed sacrament, which is the precious food of true life; and with all the sweet sacraments he sustains us most mercifully and graciously.

There is a wholeness of imagery here which goes far beyond the male-dominated concepts of God which we find in many later writers.

At this present time we are being drawn, not least by the insights of feminist theology, into a much more whole and integrated understanding of God and our relationship with God. Our thinking has been dominated by the concept of the fatherhood of God and we cannot deny the importance of this. Jesus himself called him 'Abba Father' – but God is neither male nor female; God is more than male and female; God is more than father and mother; God is more than personality. At the same time all the attributes which we discover from fatherhood and motherhood, from the fulfilment of male and female, reach their fulfilment in God. The fact that we know within ourselves and experience in our lives many failures to live up to our potential is related to the sense of integration and perfection which we can find in God alone. In a sense, the whole purpose of our search for God is the search for that wholeness which goes beyond all personality. Feminist theology – frequently drawing on mediaeval writers such as Julian and Hildegard of Bingen

– is helping us to find yet another aspect of that *Shalom* (Wholeness) which is the gift of God.

We see this in the *Anima Christi*. The word *anima* in Latin is feminine. It is interesting that when St Jerome translated the Greek New Testament into Latin for the Vulgate, he could have translated the Greek *pneuma* with the Latin *anima*. Instead, he used the male Latin noun *spiritus*. Theology might have taken a different turn if he had not done this. Certainly the implication of some parts of Scripture is to give a feminine attribution to the Spirit. This is clear in St Paul's Epistle to the Romans when, in Chapter 8, Paul speaks of the Spirit both as enabling us to cry 'Abba Father' (v. 15) and as groaning with the pangs of childbirth (vv. 22 and 23).

Modern psychology has taught us that we all have male and female elements in us. The work which has been done examining the functions of the two sides of the brain is one aspect of this. One side is more male and deductive, the other side female and intuitive. There is a need to ensure that the one side of the brain does not dominate the whole brain at the expense of the other. There is a very grave risk in our world that the mechanical, technological and deductive aspects are dominating the intuitive, artistic and aesthetic side and this is leading to warped personalities. The Church can help to redress this balance, by reasserting not just the spiritual but also the heavenly.

It is interesting that Carl Jung makes a similar point in his use of the words *animus* and *anima*. He argues that the unconscious of the male has in it the complementary element of the female – the *anima*. The female has a complementary *animus*. He writes: 'An inherited collective image of woman exists in a man's unconscious with the help of which he can apprehend the nature of woman.'

This apprehension begins with man's experience of his mother. This image is then projected on to other women. Men are often not aware of what they are projecting and

this is a major cause of difficult and disastrous relationships. Jung sees that this archetype of the *anima* in the
unconscious of the man and of the *animus* in the unconscious of the woman needs to be acknowledged and
understood. The process of the integration of a human
being, which Jung calls 'individuation', requires some
acknowledgement of these matters. Fr Christopher
Bryant, in *Jung and the Christian Way*, points out the need
to come to terms with our contrasexual nature. He sums
it up:

> The woman who identifies with her animus and allows
> it to dominate tends to be argumentative and unyield-
> ing in her assertion of views which she has not thought
> out but has gained at second hand. A man, on the
> other hand, who identifies with his anima tends to be
> effeminate and sentimental.

There are whole parts of our own nature which we need
to explore. The debate about the meaning of human
sexuality is part of the exploration and one which we find
very agonising.

This in part explains why so many people have found
the debate about the ordination of women so painful. It
is surely right that the Christian priesthood must reflect
the wholeness of humanity and the wholeness of God. If
priesthood is a representative function, then it is vital that
women are seen as part of the priesthood. If it is a way
of showing the nature of the Godhead, we are diminish-
ing that nature by denying the images of motherhood
within the Godhead. At the same time we need to realise
that this is very delicate ground.

This is an area which brings much disturbance and
fear. Male dominance is deeply embedded in our society
at almost every level and it has been given a deeper
justification in the Church through hierarchical structures and through an overemphasis on the fatherhood of
God. It comes through in priesthood as well. Someone
recently expressed this to me by saying that he had

attended a Eucharist in America celebrated by a woman priest. It all felt very different, and then he realised what it was: he summed it up in the word 'teatime'. We have been dominated by the expression of Sunday dinner presided over by the father of the house. He suddenly realised that there was another image – of 'teatime' presided over by the mother. We need both concepts and need to go beyond them.

There is a deep, almost primaeval, fear that the ordination of women is related to witchcraft, to the worship of mother earth, to fertility cults and all that is associated with them. Certainly we cannot deny that witchcraft has always been an area of female dominance, but that is probably because of the male dominance in the Church. Fred Welbourne, commenting on African independent churches, produced the adage: 'The nigger in the woodpile is there because there is no room for him in the house'. The development of an anti-Christian female priesthood outside the Church is yet another aspect of male dominance. Remove male dominance and we will have a fuller, more complete ministry, which can serve a society in which women will feel less rejected.

As we look at the Wurzburg crucifix and all that it symbolises we might well have our fears removed. The cradling arms of the bleeding Christ can take away our fears, as a mother seeks to remove a child's fears. They show us that God gives us love, support and acceptance at every stage of our life – for underneath are the everlasting arms.

Call me when my life shall fail me.

The *Anima Christi* calls us to reflect upon our death. The life we have lived, supported by the love of others, sustained by and only through the love of God, comes to an end – we die. The reality of death was something about which people of the period of Julian of Norwich knew a great deal. The Black Death had decimated the popu-

lation of Europe. There were the effects of terrible civil
strife which may be easily summed up in the fact that at
the Battle of Shrewsbury of 1403 some five thousand
young men were slain in one day. Death was an immediate
reality. How to die was something that mattered and praying for the dead a responsibility which lay on those left
behind. The selling of indulgences and the setting up of
chantry chapels to pray for the dead became a major part
of the life of the Church. Monasteries became very rich
as a result and some people set up their own colleges of
clergy to pray for the dead rather than give more money
to the monasteries. For poor people Guilds of Prayer were
set up, dedicated to prayers for the dead.

Dame Julian's visions began at a time when she thought
she was dying and it was in those visions that she saw the
great love of God. She needed to experience the suffering
to perceive the depths of God's love.

During the great carnage of the First World War there
were also those who worked their way through it to a
deeper understanding of God's love. The Revd Geoffrey
Studdert-Kennedy (Woodbine Willie) had a deep understanding of the meaning of the atonement which he often
expressed more in poetry than in sermons. This great
figure, who was an Army Chaplain and Director of the
Industrial Christian Fellowship, and burned himself out
and died at the age of forty-six, wrote wartime poetry
which spoke to the ordinary people of the deep love of
God. He saw God suffering in the suffering of the soldiers
he sought to minister to. He saw the dying Christ accepting the thief as a symbol of God's acceptance of fallen
humanity. His poem 'A Mother Understands' is both a
reflection on the *Anima Christi* and, in a way, on the
Wurzburg crucifix.

> Dear Lord, I hold my hand to take
> Thy body, broken once for me,
> Accept the Sacrifice I make,
> My body, broken, Christ, for Thee.

His was my body, born of me,
Born of my bitter travail pain
And it lies broken on the field,
Swept by the wind and the rain.

Surely a mother understands Thy thorn-crowned head
The mystery of Thy piercèd hands – the Broken Bread.

We may dimly respond to the agonies of sudden death and the air of loss, but how may we think creatively of death itself?

Jesus cries out from the Cross: 'Father into your hands I commit my spirit [*anima*]' (Luke 23:46). He surrenders his breath, his life, to God. Perhaps we see it more clearly in St John's Gospel (John 19:30), where we read how Jesus bowed his head and handed over his Spirit (*anima*). The handing over is a theme which runs through St John's Gospel – it is a symbol of the offering of God. The Greek verb here implies a genuine person offering up his Spirit to God. The whole of his life is symbolised in this offering. Pilate handed Jesus over to be crucified and now Jesus hands himself over to God. Later he hands over his Spirit to the Church. Our whole life can be summed up in the need to offer ourselves, like Christ, to God.

In his *Spiritual Exercises* St Ignatius Loyola calls upon the retreatant to kneel before the crucifix and to reflect:

> What I have done for Christ?
> What I am doing for Christ?
> What I will do for Christ?

What we discover is that God is ever calling us to himself. God yearns for us, and all our life is a call into union with God. Teilhard de Chardin in *Le Milieu Divin* has the most profound things to say about death. We are all in a process of divinisation as God calls us to himself, but we find it difficult to let go. We have to loose all footholds within ourselves and the agent of that transformation is death. 'Teach me,' he prays, 'to treat my death as an act of communion.' God will not let us go. As we go through

life resisting the call of God, we forget that God holds
the final trump card. Death is the assurance of God's
ultimate victory over our wilfulness and lack of love. Death
is the final victory: the statement, 'Father into thy hands
I commend my spirit,' and the *consummatum est* – the
triumphant 'It is finished,' – are one.

No doubt Pope Pius XII was repeating the *Anima Christi*
at his death because it was familiar to him and he had
used it for many years. The use of familiar prayers at the
time of death is a useful pastoral practice for the clergy
and indeed for anyone ministering to the dying. The
development of frequently used prayer is highly thera-
peutic. Jesus seems to have prayed Psalm 22.

My observation as a human being and as someone who
has ministered to dying people is that people die as they
have lived. Those habit-forming patterns of behaviour
and attitudes of mind which we have built up during our
lifetime condition the way we die. How we have each
developed as a person reveals itself at the time of death.
Those who have fought carry on fighting; those who have
grabbed and grasped at life continue to cling to it; those
who have learned to accept life accept death; those who
have learned the art of surrender find themselves able to
surrender to death; those whose life has been full of
agony agonise in death. The way we have learned to pray,
the way we have used the sacraments, the way we think,
become part of our dying. The inner life which we have
formed, at the point of death, forms us.

The cradling arms of the Crucified can, if we will let
them, lift us up to God. They are the sign and the symbol
of God's unconditional love and acceptance. God loves
and accepts not the good and the great, but you and me
just as we are. There are no requirements except to
respond to the love God has shown to us. So we may
hand over our *anima*, our spirit, to him who surrenders
all to God and surrenders us with him.

11

Bid me come to thee above

We saw in the introduction how one mystery play has 'Anima Christi' as the character who goes to harrow hell. The whole idea of the harrowing of hell has its origins in the verses in 1 Peter 3:18–19:

> Christ too suffered for our sins once and for all, the just for the unjust, that he might bring us to God: put to death in the body he was brought to life in the spirit. In the spirit also he went and made his proclamation to the imprisoned spirits.

The problem was how to relate the salvation wrought by Christ to those who lived before Christ – thus Christ preaching to the imprisoned spirits before he rose from the dead provided the answer. In the harrowing of hell the Redeemer defeats the devil and saves all humanity and brings us all into unity with himself.

Around this matter there still lies a great theological divide between those who hold what is usually called a universalist position and those who deny it. The universalists would argue that in Christ all humanity is redeemed. The opponents would argue rather for the reality of the devil and hell and the option for people who choose to be damned for ever. This, they would argue, is what gives urgency and bite to the preaching of the Gospel: all who do not hear and accept the Gospel are doomed for eternity. There is a middle position which is summed up in the Catholic doctrine of purgatory and expressed powerfully in Newman's *Dream of Gerontius*: all may eventually be saved but after this life all must face a period of purgatory and cleansing before they will be fit to enter into the presence of God.

The anti-universalist view tends to go along with a retributive view of the meaning of the Cross, namely that God is an angry God who cannot face sin and evil. Jesus dies on the Cross as a substitute for us and God inflicts all his judgement on him. There are many theories of the atonement. Like other Christian doctrines we are not called to accept any particular theory but to accept the principle. The themes have varied and been conditioned by the cultures from which they have emerged – for example: a view of the atonement as ransom reflects an age of slavery and a view of the Cross as a symbol of love, as seen by Abelard, reflects the emerging age of romantic love. I have expressed in Chapter 5 what seems to me to be an acceptable view of the atonement, as God taking responsibility for evil in the world. The substitutionary view is unjust and immoral. It relies on a wrathful image of God which runs counter to what we have learned in Christ. Similarly, an anti-universalistic view reads like a desperate attempt to turn the Church into a ghetto of the like-minded elite. The concept of hell is not really necessary – it could well be that an effective definition of hell is being in heaven and not wanting to be there. Heaven here is defined as the presence of God, for we can speculate as we like, but we will discover little more.

Surely the universalistic position is really the only viable one? As we have seen from St Ignatius Loyola, all that we are depends on God. God loves us and cares for us. Surely what he has created he will never reject. A God whose love does not extend to the total acceptance of all his Creation is not really a loving God. Of course, God is also a God of justice and purity, but true love does not depend upon the instilling of fear into people. The Church kept its grip on people for many centuries by the threat of hell and it enabled many people to accept terrible conditions in life by the promise of heaven. E P Thompson has analysed this in his book *The Making of the English Working Class*. The hymns and the preaching of Methodism were all geared, albeit unconsciously, to enable those already oppressed to find relief from the pains of living through religious experience. Thompson points to the use of imagery very like that in the *Anima Christi* which he sees as 'sexual and womb regressive'. This language had come into Methodism from the Moravians and was subsequently modified in later Methodism.

> O precious side hole's cavity
> I want to spend my life in thee . . .
> There is one side hole joy divine
> I'll spend all future days of mine.
> Yes, yes I will forever sit,
> There where thy side was split.

We have already seen Wesley's version of the *Anima Christi*. The following is another similar example:

> 'Tis there I would always abide,
> And never a moment depart,
> Conceal'd in the cleft of Thy side,
> Eternally held in Thy heart.

Words and phrases like this, even if used unconsciously, do point to the profound sociological effect of some forms of devotion. They show how such a prayer as the *Anima Christi* can be used to suppress and dominate the human spirit rather than liberate it. In this way people were more easily enabled to accept the injustice of their situation by catching what they saw as a glimpse of the heaven that was to await them hereafter. This emphasis on certainty and the conversion experience is to some extent a delusion. Dr William Sergeant has pointed out in his book *The Mind Possessed*:

> Wesley's own beliefs about sudden conversion were confirmed when he found that more than 600 of his followers all experienced it, and so he preached that

sudden conversion was the only sure road to salvation. Good works alone, or intellectual adherence were of no value to his vast congregations. But his converts never realised that their sudden and totally convincing state had been brought about by Wesley's own beliefs and preaching methods, which in turn, in their own way their dramatic conversions had reinforced.

This is not to say that the experience had no value, but it means that it had no ultimate value in determining the truth of what was going on. The liberation theologians are surely on firmer ground when they affirm that a spirituality which is real will express solidarity with the poor and a commitment to social justice as part of what it means to live by and proclaim the Kingdom of God.

The Church has a task to proclaim love and the justice of God. Its chief proclamation will not be in words but in the worshipping life of its members and the actions it takes within society. The preaching of hell-fire or the promise of heaven is proselytism not evangelism. Proselytism is the attempt to convert people, using means which are contrary to the Gospel. Much more care is needed about the way we communicate faith in order to build bridges to people and not to alienate them. Many have not heard the Gospel, not because of faults within themselves, but because of the Church's failure to understand them, love them and serve them. If people go to hell because they have not heard the Gospel, the Church will be in hell before them.

We have to live by and be faithful to the Gospel of the total acceptance of us by God without any strings attached. God accepts us all just as we are. Our difficulty, as Paul Tillich pointed out, is accepting the fact that we are accepted in spite of knowing that we are unacceptable.

That is how the transformation takes place. If the modern secular world finds the message hard to hear, that is no reason for Christians to give up – it is all the more reason for Christians to involve themselves in

society. We need to show love, care, forgiveness and
acceptance within it. We have to find ways of transforming
society so that human values and the love of God are
equally affirmed: they are part of the same thing. To be
concerned about our own salvation is not a Christian
virtue. Our concern should be to respond to the love of
God and leave the rest in his hands,.

A Church which is too judgemental cannot let the love
of Christ be known. A Church which sets up deep barriers
for membership, which insists that people have under-
gone the same sort of experience or come from the same
class background, is not a Church but a ghetto. Jesus
warned against being judgemental, otherwise we find ourselves as the judged. The Christian pastor and the Christian congregation know that they must let the wheat and
the tares grow together until the harvest (Matthew 13:30).
They must know that it is God's harvest and not their
own. Many who think themselves wheat will discover they
are tares and vice versa.

We cannot know whether there is a heaven or hell, but
we can be sure of the love of God. That is what drives us
on as it did St Paul: 'For the love of Christ controls
us once we have reached the conclusion that one man
has died for all therefore all mankind has died' (2 Corin-
thians 5:14). The harrowing of hell is still a helpful picture, because it reveals the universality of God's love. We
have no need of bribes or fear of threats. The hymn 'My
God I love thee, not because' sums it up:

> Then why, O blessed Jesu Christ,
> should I not love thee well?
> Not for the sake of winning heaven,
> nor of escaping hell;
>
> Not from the hope of gaining aught,
> not seeking a reward;
> But as thyself hast loved me,
> O ever-loving Lord.

So would I love thee, dearest Lord,
and in thy praise will sing;
Solely because thou art my God,
and my most loving King.

12

With thy saints to sing thy love

In Tong Church in Shropshire there is the tomb of Sir
Richard Vernon. He was at one time Speaker of the House
of Commons and before that Treasurer of Calais. He died
in the year 1451 and lies in the church beside his wife
Benedicta. The church itself had been founded by his
uncle's wife as a collegiate church to say masses for the
dead, especially for the souls of her three husbands.

The tomb is a large one. He and his wife lie on the
top, while around the base are angels holding shields and
in between them are the twelve apostles. Each apostle
holds a symbol so that we know who each one is. St Peter
has his keys, St John a chalice, St Bartholomew a knife
signifying that he was flayed alive. Sir Richard and his
wife, the tomb seems to be saying, are being held up,
sustained by the saints and angels which surround and
support them. Other tombs have Bedesmen along the
base, symbolising the prayers of the faithful.

The doctrine of the communion of saints meant a very
great deal to the mediaeval Church. The example, the
inspiration of the saints, was at one level a way of gaining
confidence in discipleship. At another level, fellowship in
the saints was an expression of the corporate nature of
the Christian faith.

The veneration and the cult of the saints in mediaeval
times went to ridiculous lengths. The collection of relics
was a way of attracting tourists and generating income for
great churches and cathedrals. Pilgrims came to witness
miracles at the shrines of saints and miracles were needed

to establish the saints' authenticity. Altars had the relics of saints within them. The lives of the saints were also a great inspiration to people to keep the faith. From the Acts of the Apostles onwards people have been inspired by the stories of what other people have done to persevere in the faith. This is not just a phenomenon of the distant past and some saints of the past, like St Francis of Assisi, seem to be very meaningful to people today. Sometimes this will be due to reading our own understanding into the lives of the saints. Thus the development of an ecological awareness is one reason why St Francis is seen as attractive today.

Possibly even more inspiring are the witnesses to the faith of our own time. The effects of the media can be to bring them to life in new ways. We can become aware of many of those who resisted Hitler, such as Bonhoeffer, Niemöller and Maximilian Kolbe. We can be inspired by those who have died in their search for human dignity and human rights, such as Martin Luther King, Janani Luwum and Oscar Romero. We are also aware of the great witness given in the care of the poor and the oppressed by Mother Teresa, C F Andrews and Fr Borelli. We can think of the defenders of human dignity and human rights like Dag Hammerskjold, Trevor Huddleston and those priests and pastors in Eastern Europe who helped bring about a new era there. We can then ask what it is that inspires them, where they draw their strength from – and we shall find that they are followers of the crucified Jesus. By examining their lives and their prayers and their writings we shall find a common source and a common inspiration.

We can also undertake a different exercise and look at great Christian figures of different ages and see what they have in common with each other. We can see how some of the same things inspire them and some of the same issues hold them together. Sometimes they have read the same books, for example Thomas à Kempis' *The Imitation of Christ*. Some of them have been inspired by the same saints of earlier ages; some of them have shared the same prayers. All of them have been part of that flow of a worshipping community which knows no boundaries in time or space. They have all found that following Christ has involved suffering. They have all found that their loyalty to Jesus has led them to make many other people uncomfortable. They have all found that they have stirred up fear and aggression in others, especially where people's vested interests and greed have been questioned. They have all posed questions in the lives of others. Their honesty has often led others to hate them. Their courage has led others to admire them.

The Epistle to the Hebrews explains the reason for this. The great cloud of witnesses (Hebrews 11 and 12) are following Jesus (Joshua), he who goes ahead and is the pioneer, who blazes the trail to open up a new way to God. Christians never simply look back, they also look forward. They are willing to ask questions where others simply accept tradition. They can do this because they know that, wherever they go, Jesus has gone before. There is no area of life that cannot be questioned, no peak that cannot be climbed, no depths that cannot be probed. Jesus is always before them and as they look to him he takes them outside the camp, he leads them where others are fearful to go. The Psalmist was also sure of this, as we saw in Bishop Jeremy Taylor's use of verses 7 and 8 of Psalm 139 in Chapter 8. It is one of the ways in which we express our Resurrection faith. Jesus goes before us into Galilee (Mark 16:7).

The fellowship of the saints is a fellowship of questioners, experimenters and explorers. If they had not been, life would not have changed: we would still be accepting the world view, the social conditions, the slavery and the oppression of the New Testament world. Not all change may be attributed to Christian people, but take them away and history would be a lot less interesting. We cannot go back, but we can go marching on with the saints.

There is another aspect. As we have confidence to
follow in the footsteps of others we need to remember
another word from the writer to the Hebrews. It is that
'They without us cannot be made perfect' (Hebrews
11:40). There is an intertwining and an interdependence
within the whole body of Christ which we have not yet
fully grasped. It is something which again goes against
the spirit of our own age. Holy Scripture gives us a picture
of a tribal, mutually supportive, sharing community. We
can still see this in parts of Africa and Asia. The family is
not a small nuclear unit of mother, father and two
children living in an isolated, self-supportive lifestyle. This
nuclear family, as we all know, is a major force of disinte-
gration within our society. The biblical family is large – it
runs through several generations and through layers of
relatives who all help and share with each other. The
Church has done itself a great disservice in the West by
talking about family services and family Communion. It
reflects the small nuclear family and often also hints at
male domination ('Father knows best'). It also falls into
the hands of the views of the world around us. Our society
is full of the policies of competition and the economics
of the trade war. It is a world for asserting individual
rights and proclaiming that there is no such thing as
community. Such views do not blend well with a doctrine
of the communion of saints, because their motive and
end are very different. The end of the communion of
saints is not personal satisfaction or even personal salvation. The end is the corporate harmony of all things
existing within the praise, worship and adoration of an
everlasting God.

Our God has cradling arms and his hands are pierced
with nails. Our God shares our sufferings and is
crowned with thorns.

Our God reigns from the tree and opens the way to
glory.

We now turn to the praise and worship of God. There
have been some very sombre themes running through

this book. This has been done much to try and redress the balance from the very hedonistic world in which we live today, but it would be wrong to leave it there.

All the way through we have been reflecting the mind and life of the mediaeval Church with our own. In the matter of worship the mediaeval Church was very colourful and, while the reformers thought much of it led to excessive diversity, not to say idolatry, it did have a lot to commend it. The mediaeval Church was dealing with a mainly illiterate people, whereas the Renaissance and the Reformation were the fruits of growing literacy. The mediaeval Church had to find ways of expressing the faith and communicating Christian truth to people who were not able to read the Scriptures or think in a literary way. Mystery plays were one way of trying to relate the Gospel story to people's own daily life. Processions and ceremonies throughout the year were there to involve people in festivity and community sharing. Wall paintings, be it of the Pantocrator or the torments of hell, were there to remind people of Christian doctrine and the dominance of the Church. The celebration of the Mass, accompanied by music, lights, incense and ceremony, was there to help people enter into an understanding of the mystery of God. Admittedly there was also a not inconsiderable element of keeping the people in their place and asserting the domination of the Church, but there was a good side to it as well.

The teaching of simple prayers like the *Anima Christi* to use at certain stages of the Mass was a way of teaching people devotion. In a world where the Church was dominant, much Church life provided variety and excitement during a drab existence. People who moved little and worked in one locality were at the mercy of their feudal lords. Liturgy was fun and, not least in the events of Holy Week, much was done to draw people in. Think of the choristers at Salisbury throwing buns to the people from a raised platform on Palm Sunday; think of the drama of Tenebrae as all the lights gradually went out on the early days of Holy Week; or of the watch at the Easter sepulchre from Good Friday to Easter Sunday. Visual aids abounded and there was frequently a sense of festivity.

The Anglo-Catholic clergy working in places like the East End of London in the second half of the nineteenth century sought to bring back this joy, colour and ceremonial for the people. Some clergy were persecuted for it. They may have been mistaken to some extent, as Owen Chadwick has pointed out, for it was really the quality of the pastoral care and the lives of the priests which communicated itself. The people supported their priests because they were holy men, not because of the ceremonial in the churches, much of which they did not understand.

Nevertheless, we do need a real understanding of the meaning of worship within the life of the Church. The key to that understanding lies in the realisation that worship is play. We come to this by seeing first of all that Creation is play. God did not need to create the world. If he had needed to he would have been driven by some power greater than himself, and that is not possible. So Jürgen Moltmann expresses it:

> When he creates something that is not God but also not nothing, this must have its ground not in itself but in God's good will and pleasure. Hence the Creation is God's play, a play of his groundless and inscrutable wisdom. It is the realm in which God displays his glory.

It was Joseph Pieper, in his seminal essay 'Leisure as the basis of Culture', who pointed out that it is leisure which enables us to accept the reality of the Creation. Leisure is not simply non-activity: its roots lie in celebration, in contemplation, in games, feasts and reflections. Pieper notes: 'In leisure the truly human values are saved and preserved because leisure is the means whereby the sphere of the specific human can over and again be left behind.' Thus leisure may be contrasted to some extent with work on one side, but on the other side with laziness, which is non-productive and non-reflective. It is what the Greeks called *accidie*, despair, or, as Kierkegaard put it, 'a despairing refusal to be oneself'. Much of the modern leisure industry panders to this aspect of modern life. It leads to a despairing attitude where people no longer believe in the power to transform things. Creativity is stultified and realised with a negative passivity. What is needed in our society is creative play. It is not only children who need to, or indeed do, play. Much of life is made up of ritualised games, which we play with each other. Ruben Alves thinks that children's games are more creative than adult games. Children feel free to enter in and out of their games, change the rules when they want to and even change roles all the time. Adults, on the contrary, like to think that their games are reality and that rules must be observed and roles cannot be changed. Ruben Alves concludes: 'Children's play ends with universal resurrection of the dead. Adults' play ends with universal burial. Whereas the resurrection is the paradigm of the world of children the world of adults creates the Cross.'

John Huizinga has shown that play is the basic experience of humanity. Games will be played everywhere. They provide an alternative world with its own rules. Peter Berger has pointed out that games have their own internal logic which is unrelated to the world outside and we are free to move from one to the other. Play is a joyful activity and if it stops being joyful we just give it up. Play is always an essential part of learning and maturing. Thus we may describe worship as a focal point of play where we share in God's creative play. In sacramental worship the full power of worship is realised as we are caught up into another dimension and we cross the frontiers of our daily life into God's playful activity. It does not deny our daily life or our history. The sacrament is the way through to a world of ecstasy whereby we contact the heavenly.

Worship also helps us to relate to the secular society in which we are placed. The very fact that most of life has set itself free from the dominance of the Church can set the Church free to be itself and to worship God for God's sake, thereby asserting a different level of priorities in the world. Moltmann sees this as liberating religion, God and faith from being helpers or supports to us. They can now be themselves again.

For far too long we have been using God to enable us to survive in the world. Now we have the chance to use the world to enjoy God. We can cease using God as a helper in need, a God of the gaps, or a problem solver. We are free for the joy of God and the enjoyment of God in each other. Few in the Church have yet seen that liberation. The Church still spends a great deal of time justifying itself in terms of service to the community. This is not to say that there is no social role for the Church, but seeing that new-found freedom makes service in life much easier. Moreover, Christians should seek to develop forms of leisure which are non-exploitative of people in society. We need to be helping people to find space just to be. Moltmann talks about the Church as the 'congregation of the liberated'. It has to affirm the value just of being. Worship as play points to the transcendence of God in our midst and the possibility of much creativity. If this really is the case, then our liturgical reforms have hardly started. Again we must be careful, for we have no need to reject the insight into worship of our predecessors. We need to carry them forward into the creative play which will be infectious for people today. The great interest in art, theatre and culture of our own time provides us with the clue.

The infectious and converting effect of worship as play is demonstrated very vividly in the life of George Macleod, the founder of the Iona Community. At Easter 1933 he attended a Russian Orthodox Easter Service in Jerusalem. It changed his life. The moment when the priests rushed out crying 'Christ is Risen' and all followed with lighted candles was a moment of revelation. The service lasted three and a half hours and this Presbyterian minister was spellbound. He wrote of it:

> For sheer worship I have never seen anything like it – nor shall see again on earth – we can never touch it in the West – not even Rome could do it. It was the devotional presentation of the New Life, beyond acting and beyond 'Lesson' – simply worship – It was the earnest that Bolshevism must pass. There was more Reality in the Patriarch's little finger than in Stalin's whole council assembled.

It was for Macleod a second conversion. His biographer states that through it he rediscovered a sense of the Church as the corporate Body of Christ.

The Iona Community was in many ways the working out of this vision in action. Such can be the power of creative play and positive worship. We need much more joy like this in our churches.

At the very heart of our faith is creative joy, which we share with all who have gone before us and with whom we still share within the heavens. Thus there is joy at the heart of God – the deepest meaning of life is not suffering but celebration. The joy in heaven is reflected in the worship of humanity on earth. The Orthodox Churches have much to teach the more cerebral West about the ongoing worship of God. We are caught up into the very heart of God where suffering and joy become one. Our life, our prayer and our pain are lost in the totally enveloping, overwhelming love of God.

We can still pray the *Anima Christi*. We may have changed its emphasis and significance, but within it we find a tradition which looks to the past and gives us a spirituality which moves to the future.

Conclusion

In 1987, during investigations to look at the base of the tower piers of Worcester Cathedral, workmen came across a pair of feet sticking out of the ground. A thorough archaeological investigation ensued and uncovered a man dressed as a pilgrim. Alongside him was his pilgrim's staff. He had with him palms signifying that he had been to Jerusalem and a cockle shell from Compostella. If you visit the Cathedral now you will find his boots and his staff on display in the Crypt. He symbolises the thousands of pilgrims who came to Worcester in the Middle Ages. They came to visit the shrines of St Oswald, St Wulstan and Our Lady of Worcester.

This book has been an attempt to relate mediaeval prayer and aspects of mediaeval faith to the sort of faith we need in the world today. The language of pilgrimage provides a thread which runs right through. The language of pilgrimage has become very popular in the Church since the Second Vatican Council. It is an appropriate image of the Church in an age when travel is easy, migrant workers a common phenomenon and life changes rapidly. The picture of a Church on the move, travelling light, unencumbered with too much baggage, is a helpful one. It is also a thoroughly biblical picture. The people of God have been on the move from the days of the Exodus. The Gospel is and has been preached in a variety of places and contexts and there is an inevitable interaction of the context on the way the Gospel is communicated.

There are many today who would call us to be faithful

to the tradition which was once delivered to the saints. They do not realise what they are saying. The way the faith is interpreted changes from age to age. Just to compare the world view of the fourteenth century with that of the twentieth century makes this very apparent. At the same time, to reject what we have received from the past would be totally wrong because by so doing we would be rejecting all the benefits which people have received. The image of pilgrimage may help: we are a people on the move; we bring with us the traditions of the past. They are our source and resource material. We can probe them and find much that is of value, albeit reinterpreted in some way or another.

Christians are people who must ask questions and face new issues. That is part of their tradition – it is what Christians have always done. The great commission to go out in love and preach the Gospel (Matthew 28:19) means that all the time we are probing and trying to make connections with the world around us. We cannot do this without the tradition behind us. At the same time we cannot do it without changing the tradition. Just as we make our own Gospel stories in our lives and hear them in the lives of others, so we not only inherit tradition, we also make it.

The Church and the faith are ever in a process of change and development. If it is living it cannot be otherwise. There are various strands which interact to enable this to happen: there is the word of Scripture, an essential element which we share and use; there is the worshipping tradition of the Church which grows and changes within the culture where it is set; there is the reflection on the Gospel and tradition which emerges out of our corporate and individual experience. This experience includes both our life of prayer and the questions – moral, personal and social – which we encounter in our daily living. All this is being woven together. Tradition is like a three-dimensional tapestry to which we are all adding a small bit in our own day – thus we are contributing to that wholeness and fullness which is the promise of God and which we shall never fully see.

Such a view of tradition is possible if we hold to a perception of a God who is continuously active in every aspect of life in the world. We have seen all the way through these reflections that the division of sacred and secular is false. Everything we do and every encounter we have has within it the challenge of God. We cannot denigrate the past – we have to try and perceive what God has been and is saying through it. We need the measure of Scripture, reason, tradition and experience to see how this relates to God's purposes. We shall make mistakes as our forebears made mistakes, but that is not a reason for giving up the attempt to reinterpret the faith for our age.

The way of faith is a risky business – there are no certainties to hide behind. There is a way of life inspired by what we have received, lived out in the present and held together by the judging and loving activities of God which pervade everything. Christian people are a pilgrim people, they are on a journey. They are not full of certainties and they never know what will happen next. But pilgrims are not alone: with them are the pilgrims who have gone before and those who follow after, as well as those who travel with them. Many of our fellow pilgrims will perceive things in a different way, but we need each other on the journey.

Our pilgrimage is itself an act of faith and an act of worship. We are moving towards the greater mystery of God which envelops us all.

Pilgrims live only by the mercy and grace of God. This means that we can let go of security and certainties because we realise that God is in control. We need nothing but to offer everything to God with willingness. That is the way of the *Anima Christi*.